STRATEGY 2030 ENERGY SECTOR DIRECTIONAL GUIDE

INCLUSIVE, JUST, AND AFFORDABLE LOW-CARBON TRANSITION IN ASIA AND THE PACIFIC

JULY 2023

ASIAN DEVELOPMENT BANK

ADB

CONTENTS

TABLES AND FIGURES

ABBREVIATIONS

ADB	Asian Development Bank
CCUS	carbon capture, use, and storage
CO_2	carbon dioxide
COP 21	Twenty-First Session of the Conference of the Parties
COVID-19	coronavirus disease
CPS	country partnership strategy
CRF	corporate results framework
DMC	developing member country
ESDG	Energy Sector Directional Guide
ETM	Energy Transition Mechanism
GHG	greenhouse gas
IEA	International Energy Agency
IED	Independent Evaluation Department
LNG	liquefied natural gas
MDB	multilateral development bank
NDC	nationally determined contribution
OMDP	Office of Markets Development and Public–Private Partnership
OPs	operational priorities (1-7) of ADB Strategy 2030
PPP	public–private partnership
PSOD	Private Sector Operations Department
SDG	Sustainable Development Goal
T&D	transmission and distribution

EXECUTIVE SUMMARY

This Energy Sector Directional Guide (ESDG) provides the strategic direction of the Asian Development Bank (ADB) for the energy sector. It describes the context and rationale that will guide ADB's agenda in supporting developing member countries (DMCs) with financing, knowledge, convening ability, and technical assistance to ensure improved coherence, relevance, efficiency, and effectiveness of ADB's energy sector investments. It is intended for both an internal ADB audience (e.g., energy and other sector and department staff) and an external audience (e.g., DMC governments, line ministries, multilateral development banks, United Nations agencies, and other international entities). The ESDG aligns with Strategy 2030 and its seven operational priorities (OPs)—OP1: Addressing remaining poverty and reducing inequality; OP2: Accelerating progress in gender equality; OP3: Tackling climate change, building climate and disaster resilience, and enhancing environmental sustainability; OP4: Making cities more livable; OP5: Promoting rural development and food security; OP6: Strengthening governance and institutional capacity; and OP7: Fostering regional cooperation and integration. The ESDG assesses the current energy sector trends, challenges, and opportunities, and how ADB can best position itself to add value to energy sector development in the Asia and Pacific region. The guide also outlines the priorities and focus for the energy sector in line with ADB's Strategy 2030 published in 2018. It aims to support ADB staff in conducting energy sector operations in line with the Energy Policy 2021 up to 2030. The five policy principles of the Energy Policy 2021 are also the foundations of this ESDG and comprise the ESDG's vision and approach.

The ESDG implementation period will be from 2022 to 2030, which aligns with ADB's Strategy 2030. The directional guide is designed to be a living document, to be updated as needed, to remain relevant to the dynamic energy context of Asia and the Pacific. A midterm review will be conducted following the expected review of the Energy Policy in 2025.

Where We Are

Energy is essential to human lives. Energy services enabled by modern technologies in both rural and urban environments have a major impact on people's livelihoods. While the burden of energy poverty continues to fall most heavily on women and vulnerable people, progress on energy access has improved socioeconomic conditions like increasing agricultural and industrial productivity, increasing household income, and enhancing people's lives through increased time in doing gainful work among men and women and study time of children.

Energy cuts across all aspects of development and is essential to inclusive socioeconomic development and gender equality. As such, energy plays an important role in supporting the development of other sectors such as agriculture, education, health, transport, urban and water.

On the other hand, energy production and consumption are responsible for almost three-quarters of global greenhouse gas (GHG) emissions. This places the energy sector at the forefront of global efforts to address the impact of energy use on climate and environment.

ADB's energy sector operations have played a substantial role in delivering energy access, contributing to economic development, and improving lives throughout the region. However, achieving universal energy access to a reliable, efficient, and affordable energy supply across the region, and supporting a low-carbon transition still requires mobilizing substantial efforts and resources.

The sector-wide evaluation in 2020 by ADB's Independent Evaluation Department (IED) found that ADB's 2009 Energy Policy had been aligned with the needs of the energy sectors in DMCs and Strategy 2020 and was relevant to the ADB program during the review period. However, the 2009 Energy Policy was no longer aligned with the Sustainable Development Goals, the Paris Agreement, and ADB's Strategy 2030, thus needing an update.

ADB's Energy Policy 2021 was approved in October 2021. The vision of ADB's Energy Policy 2021 is "supporting low-carbon transition in Asia and the Pacific." The objectives of the sector operations are (i) to help ADB's DMCs accelerate the development of sustainable and resilient energy systems that provide reliable and affordable access for all, (ii) foster inclusive and environmentally sustainable economic growth and social development, and (iii) support the low-carbon transition in Asia and the Pacific.

Where We Want to Be

The energy landscape has changed radically over the last decade. The Sustainable Development Goals (established in 2015), the Paris Agreement on climate change (adopted in 2015), and ADB's Strategy 2030 set ambitious targets for providing reliable energy access to all, and amplified the calls for action on climate change.

The main challenges and emerging needs for DMCs in the energy sector still lie in ensuring (i) universal access to electricity, and clean cooking, heating, and cooling options for all households; (ii) energy security to support economic growth; (iii) sustainability across the dimensions of financial viability, effective operation and maintenance of infrastructure, resilience to climate change and extreme events, climate mitigation via lower carbon use, health, and environmental impacts; and (iv) sector governance, including regulations, utilities' performance, and private sector participation.

There have been many and fundamental changes in the energy landscape in the past decade, notably the global commitment to universal energy access and climate change, the rapid development in renewable energy, low-carbon technologies, and digital and smart technologies. In the same decade, there have been significant advances in economic development and energy modernization in Asia and the Pacific. Consolidating achievements, addressing emerging challenges and opportunities, and ensuring a just and equitable transition to a low-carbon future in Asia and the Pacific will require ADB's continued support for its DMCs on a broad range of energy issues.

To achieve the energy sector vision and objectives, ADB's Energy Policy 2021 was developed based on the following five principles:

(i)   Supporting efforts to bring affordable, reliable, sustainable, and modern energy to all, to eradicate extreme poverty and reduce social inequalities;

(ii)   Supporting DMCs to tackle climate change, enhance environmental sustainability, and build climate and disaster resilience;

(iii) Supporting the institutional development, financial sustainability, and good governance of energy sector institutions, companies, and the private sector; and assisting in creating the policy frameworks needed to manage the energy transition;

(iv)   Promoting regional energy cooperation and the integration of energy systems to strengthen energy security and increase cross-border access to cleaner energy sources; and

(v)   Continuing to combine finance, knowledge, partnerships, and its country-focused approach to deliver integrated solutions with comprehensive and magnified development impacts.

Recognizing the massive financing needs in the energy sector across the region, ADB's resources must be prioritized to tackle the most demanding energy challenges. ADB's assistance will focus on meeting emerging needs and adding value to the clients in the region. The areas of delivery will focus on the "4Ds"—decarbonization, decreasing energy intensity, digitalization, and decentralization.

ADB will facilitate the low-carbon transition by assisting its DMCs in (i) accelerating the deployment of renewable energy, (ii) pursuing strategic decarbonization and the phase-out of coal while ensuring a just transition, (iii) developing policies and regulations to support low-carbon technologies, and (iv) introducing market-based instruments including carbon pricing.

Likewise, ADB will support its DMCs in increasing energy efficiency investments to reduce energy intensity and expand energy productivity. ADB will support demand-side energy efficiency planning and implementation and promote minimum energy performance standards for appliances and equipment, fuel economy standards for vehicles, standards for electric motors in industry, mandatory energy audits, and energy management policies for large industrial and commercial companies and building codes.

ADB will help deploy digital technologies such as smart meters to reduce technical and commercial losses and encourage demand-side energy efficiency, peer-to-peer trading using blockchain technology for energy markets, and artificial intelligence for predictive grid management and grid resilience.

ADB will support low-carbon, decentralized technologies such as distributed generation, renewable energy-based micro and/or mini-grids, home systems, and energy storage systems. It will also support increased competition and private sector participation in DMCs' energy markets to contribute greater dynamism to the energy sector and take advantage of opportunities created by new technologies and business models.

This ESDG adopts a common but differentiated approach in line with each DMC's level of economic development, resource endowment, respective capabilities, and nationally determined low-carbon transition pathway.

The energy sector will prioritize essential energy access in the poorest and most vulnerable countries through greater use of low-carbon and renewable energy sources and rehabilitate infrastructure to enhance energy security and climate resilience. In low-income and lower-middle-income countries, ADB will continue to support reforms in the energy sector, including reforms of state-owned enterprises; the development of green and inclusive energy infrastructure to enhance productivity and competitiveness; the promotion of gender equality; and greater participation of the private sector in delivering energy infrastructure and services.

What We Will Do

ADB will promote poverty reduction, sustainable and inclusive growth, and regional integration, and facilitate a just low-carbon energy transition in Asia and the Pacific. As a trusted development partner, ADB will combine finance, knowledge, and partnerships to optimize its value addition in its support to sustainable development priorities of its DMCs.

In accordance with the Energy Policy 2021, ADB's energy sector operations will support energy access, energy security, environmental sustainability, and sector governance to strengthen the energy sector of the region. In particular, implementation of the Energy Policy 2021 will focus on the following:

(i)   confronting climate change by facilitating a just low-carbon energy transition through a common but differentiated approach and integrated energy planning;

(ii)   supporting DMCs in implementing just energy transition and innovative Energy Transition Mechanisms;

(iii) expanding support for demand-side energy efficiency including demand–response;

(iv)   supporting digitalization and smart power systems for increased clean energy deployment including demand–response and efficient power system management; and

(v)   leveraging advanced clean energy technologies and commercial financing to accelerate the energy transition through the One ADB approach, innovative financing mechanisms and business models, and decentralized energy systems.

WHERE WE ARE

Energy is essential to human lives and has a significant impact on almost every aspect of life. Energy provides quality services for the daily functioning of people's lives, economic activities, and public services. Energy is also essential to inclusive socioeconomic development and gender equality, related to every aspect of development. As such, energy plays an important role in supporting development of other sectors, such as agriculture, education, health, transport, urban and water. In fact, per capita energy consumption has been an important development indicator.

Energy services enabled by modern technologies in both rural and urban environments have a major impact on people's daily lives. While the burden of energy poverty continues to fall most heavily on women and vulnerable people, progress on energy access improved socioeconomic conditions like increasing agricultural and industrial productivity, increasing household income, and enhancing people's lives through increased time in doing gainful work among men and women and study time of children. Moreover, the coronavirus disease (COVID-19) pandemic has highlighted the critical need for electricity access to support related necessities such as health care and hospitals. Access to reliable electricity is critical in the transportation, distribution, and storage of vaccines, which will be instrumental in ending the COVID-19 crisis.

On the other hand, energy production and consumption are responsible for almost three-quarters of the world's greenhouse gas (GHG) emissions, which places the energy sector at the forefront of global efforts to address the impact of energy use on climate and environment. The current energy crisis has also placed energy security and energy affordability at the forefront of national priorities.

The energy sector operations of the Asian Development Bank (ADB) have played a substantial role in delivering energy access contributing to economic development and improving lives throughout the region. However, achieving universal energy access to a reliable, efficient, and affordable energy supply across the region and supporting a low-carbon transition still require mobilizing substantial efforts and resources.

The mission of ADB's Energy Policy 2021 is "supporting low-carbon transition in Asia and the Pacific." The objectives of the sector operations are to help developing member countries (DMCs) accelerate the development of sustainable and resilient energy systems that provide reliable and affordable access for all, foster inclusive economic growth and social development, and support the low-carbon transition in Asia and the Pacific.

The Energy Sector Directional Guide (ESDG) aligns with Strategy 2030 and its seven operational priorities (OPs)—OP1: Addressing remaining poverty and reducing inequality; OP2: Accelerating progress in gender equality; OP3: Tackling climate change, building climate and disaster resilience, and enhancing environmental sustainability; OP4: Making cities more livable; OP5: Promoting rural development and food security; OP6: Strengthening governance and institutional capacity; and OP7: Fostering regional cooperation and integration. The ESDG is volume 2 in the 7-volume *Strategy 2030 Sector Directional Guides* collection. The other volumes in this collection are Education Sector Directional Guide (volume 1), Finance Sector Directional Guide (volume 3), Health Sector Directional Guide (volume 4), Transport Sector Directional Guide (volume 5), Urban Sector Directional Guide (volume 6), and Water Sector Directional Guide (volume 7). The ESDG assesses the current energy sector trends, challenges, and opportunities, and how ADB can best position itself to add value to energy sector development in the Asia and Pacific region. It aims to support Asian Development Bank (ADB) staff in conducting energy sector operations in line with the Energy Policy 2021 up to 2030. The five policy principles of the Energy Policy 2021 are also the foundations of this ESDG and comprise its vision and approach. The ESDG is a living document, which will be updated as required from time to time.

A. Status of ADB's Energy Sector Operations

During 2011–2021, ADB approved $39.2 billion in financing for the energy sector, making it the second-largest sector in terms of volume of ADB support, after transport. The energy sector shares 20% of ADB lending during this period. Total approvals in electricity transmission and distribution (T&D) accounted for 48% of the total portfolio. About 52% of the portfolio is invested in clean energy, including renewable energy, energy efficiency, and fuel switching to cleaner energy.

Sovereign lending and grants accounted for three-quarters of ADB's support. Nonsovereign lending accounted for one-quarter and increased considerably during 2015–2019. Figure 1 shows the energy sector portfolio, while Figure 2 shows the sector lending by operations and Figure 3 the sector lending by subsectors between 2011–2021.

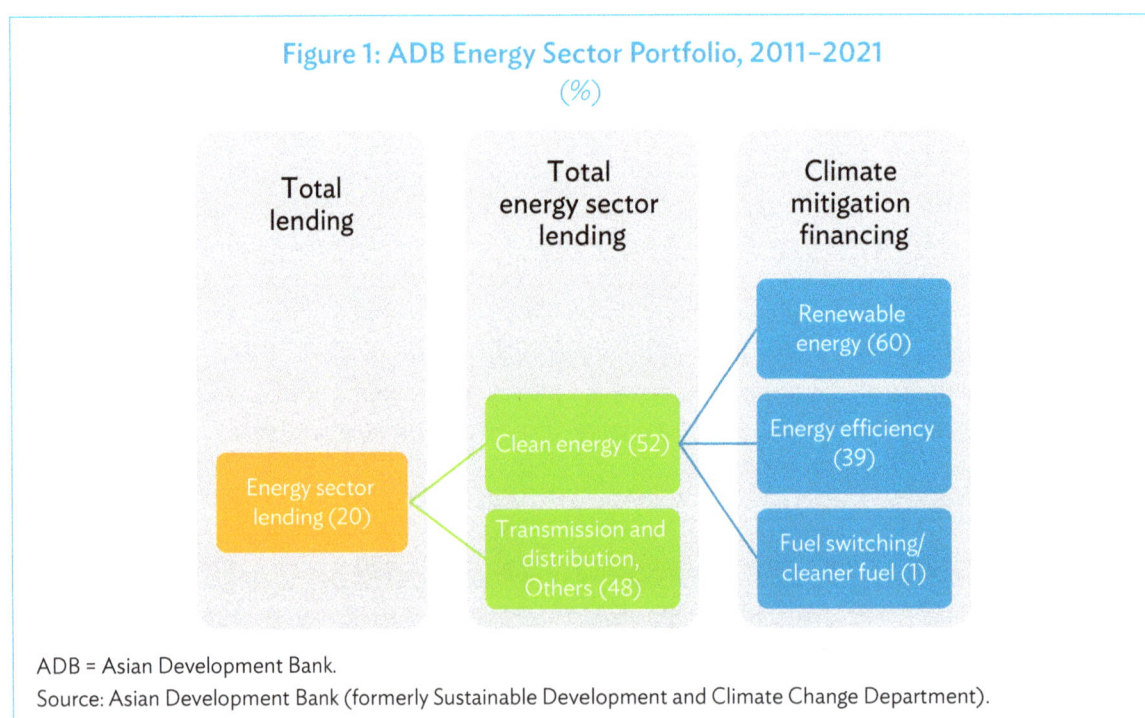

Figure 1: ADB Energy Sector Portfolio, 2011–2021
(%)

ADB = Asian Development Bank.
Source: Asian Development Bank (formerly Sustainable Development and Climate Change Department).

Figure 2: ADB Energy Sector Lending by Operations, 2011–2021
($ million)

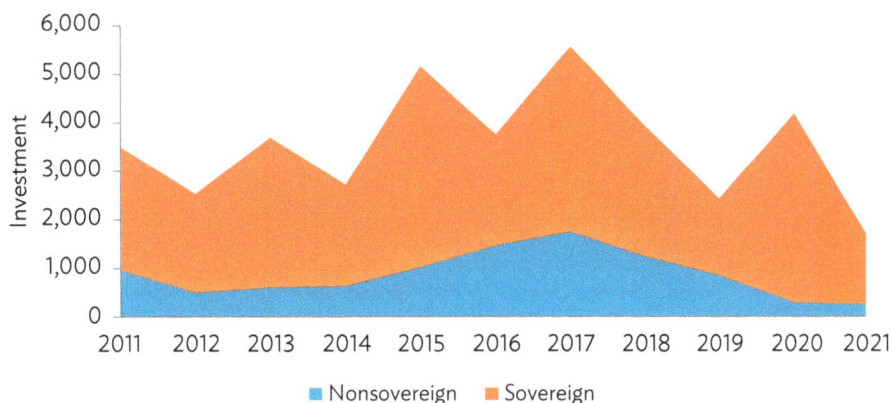

ADB = Asian Development Bank.
Source: Asian Development Bank (formerly Sustainable Development and Climate Change Department).

Figure 3: ADB Energy Sector Lending by Subsector, 2011–2021
($ million)

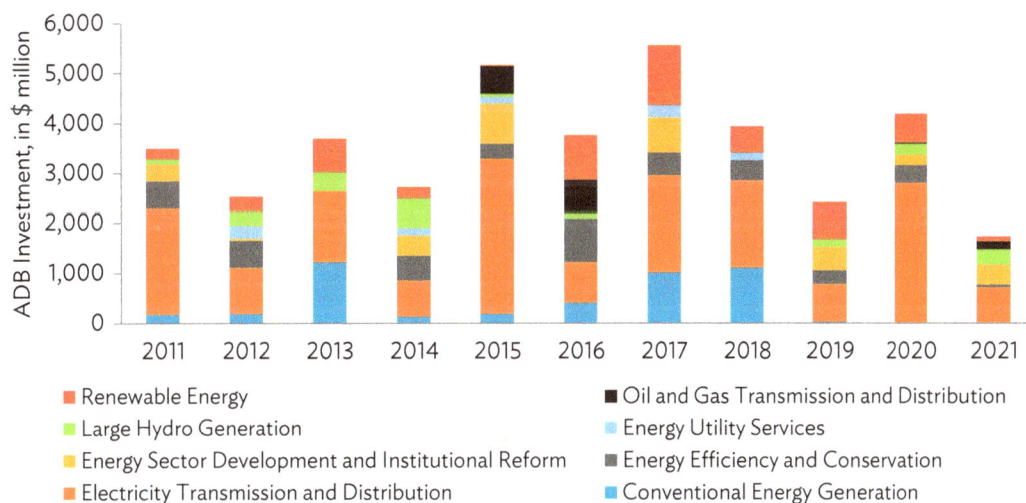

- Renewable Energy
- Large Hydro Generation
- Energy Sector Development and Institutional Reform
- Electricity Transmission and Distribution
- Oil and Gas Transmission and Distribution
- Energy Utility Services
- Energy Efficiency and Conservation
- Conventional Energy Generation

ADB = Asian Development Bank.
Source: ADB (formerly Sustainable Development and Climate Change Department).

B. The Energy Sector Review

In 2020, ADB's Independent Evaluation Department (IED) comprehensively reviewed ADB's 2009 Energy Policy and its energy operations during 2009–2019.[1] The IED evaluation highlighted significant successes in ADB's energy sector operations and found that the 2009 Energy Policy had been aligned with the needs of the energy sectors in DMCs, Strategy 2020, approaches of other multilateral development banks, climate change priorities at that time, and relevant to the ADB program during the review period.

However, IED also determined that the 2009 Energy Policy was no longer adequately aligned with the global consensus on climate change, the ongoing global transformation of the energy sector, gender equality goals, and recent changes in the energy sectors of DMCs. The Paris Agreement of 2015, the Sustainable Development Goals (SDGs), recent technological developments, and ADB's Strategy 2030 have created new conditions and demands for ADB's energy sector assistance.[2] Although ADB has not financed investments in coal-fired power plants since 2013—even as the 2009 Energy Policy allowed such financing—the current energy and climate change contexts present the opportunity and rationale to support the phase-out of coal-fired power plants in the region.

The IED evaluation recommended updates that consider the opportunities provided by innovative technologies, price dynamics, decentralized energy systems, digitalization, energy efficiency, and new business models for enhancing sustainability, resilience, inclusiveness, and energy access and security. IED also proposed that guidance on energy sector operations be updated more frequently.[3]

C. Challenges and Emerging Needs in the Energy Sector

The main challenges for DMCs in the energy sector still lie in ensuring (i) universal access to electricity, and clean cooking, heating, and cooling options for all households; (ii) energy security to support economic growth; (iii) sustainability across the dimensions of financial viability, effective operation and maintenance of infrastructure, resilience to climate change and extreme events, climate mitigation via lower carbon use, health, and environmental impacts; and (iv) sector governance, including regulations, utilities' performance, and private sector participation. While many DMCs have made significant progress in these areas, they need continued support in consolidating achievements and addressing emerging challenges and opportunities.

1. Energy Access

Progress on access to energy has been rapid across developing Asia and the Pacific, reaching an overall electrification rate of 96% in 2019, or a 16% increase since 2010. However, the electrification rates of individual DMCs vary widely and many power systems continue to be hampered by unreliable supply. Currently, about 940 million people in Asia and the Pacific still experience frequent interruptions, about 350 million people do not enjoy an adequate supply, and

---

[1]   ADB. 2009. *Energy Policy.* Manila.

[2]   ADB. 2018. *Strategy 2030: Achieving a Prosperous, Inclusive, Resilient, and Sustainable Asia and the Pacific.* Manila.

[3]   ADB. 2020. *Sector-wide Evaluation: ADB's 2009 Energy Policy and Program, 2009–2019.* Manila.

about 150 million people still have no access to electricity.[4] The issue of how to achieve adequate, reliable, and affordable universal access will therefore remain on the agendas of governments as well as national and international development financing institutions.

On the other hand, access to clean fuels and technologies for cooking, heating, and cooling remains a challenge for many DMCs in both rural and urban areas. Cooking with traditional fuels such as wood, charcoal, and animal manure is a major source of indoor air pollution and associated health problems. DMCs in the region are not on track to meet the target of universal access to clean cooking by 2030 because 1.6 billion people still have no such access, representing 43% of the population in the region. Since these impacts disproportionately burden women and children, lack of access to sustainable cooking solutions is also a social problem.

Persistent and widespread unequal access to energy services makes it imperative to prioritize support to all disadvantaged and vulnerable groups—women, the poor, racial and ethnic minorities, indigenous peoples, people with disabilities, older persons, and other marginalized people. Women in rural areas are particularly and disproportionally affected by the lack of access to clean and modern energy services. Achieving energy access in an equitable manner therefore still requires mobilizing substantial efforts and resources.

Some DMCs will still need support on the extension of the distribution grid to advance energy access, while many other countries have now shifted to reaching remote areas through off-grid solutions such as mini-grids, which need affordable, innovative, renewable energy-based mini or microgrids and sustainable business models.

2.   *Energy Security*

In addition to energy access, developing member countries need to ensure energy security to support continued economic expansion and meet demand from population growth and urbanization. The population of the Asia and Pacific region increased by 1.7% per year from 1990 to 2019, and urbanization accelerated from 36% in 1990 to 51% in 2019. The region's gross domestic product, in constant prices, grew by an average 6% per year from 1990 to 2019, while its primary energy supply increased by about 4% per year in the same period.[5]

Continuing economic growth and urbanization will require the development of affordable and reliable energy systems with substantial additional electricity-generating capacity, and flexible power systems that can balance fluctuations in demand and supply. Based on the sustainable development scenario of the International Energy Agency (IEA), installed electricity-generating capacity would increase by about 7% per year, from 3,386 gigawatts in 2019 to 6,113 gigawatts in 2030. In particular, the capacity of solar, wind, and hydropower will grow at a rate of 11% per year.[6] Accordingly, the Asia and Pacific region's investments in renewable energy generation by 2030 could reach $1.3 trillion per year, doubling the amount from the previous decade.[7]

---

[4]   International Energy Agency. 2020. World Energy Outlook 2020: Access to Electricity Database (accessed 29 April 2022).

[5]   United Nations Economic and Social Commission for Asia and the Pacific (UNESCAP). 2021. *Asia Pacific Energy Portal*. Bangkok.

[6]   IEA. 2020. *World Energy Outlook*. Paris.

[7]   UNESCAP. 2021. *Regional Trends Report: Shaping a Sustainable Energy Future in Asia and the Pacific*. Bangkok.

Such a rapid expansion of renewable energy capacity would require strong, resilient, and flexible T&D systems that allow the DMCs to increase reliability; manage variability; balance network capabilities across appropriate geographic scales, including cross-border interconnections; and adopt appropriate grid management solutions such as digitalization and storage technologies. Current investments in the region's electricity grid systems—including T&D and energy storage—are estimated to total about $1 trillion per year. ADB has extensive experience and will continue to facilitate and support cross-border power trade (among others) and investments in electricity generation, transmission infrastructure, and institutional arrangements across DMCs, including intraregional and subregional interconnections, particularly those within Central Asia, South Asia, and Southeast Asia.

3. *Environmental Sustainability*

ADB's long-term corporate strategy (Strategy 2030) stresses that ADB's vision of a prosperous, inclusive, resilient, and sustainable Asia and the Pacific hinges on the success of the region in tackling climate change, enhancing environmental sustainability and building climate and disaster resilience, and ADB's Climate Change Operational Framework sets out how ADB will support increased resilience and enhanced mitigation.[8] While DMCs did not contribute to the majority of historic emissions that have led to the current climate crisis, their emissions are now significant, and they are among the most vulnerable to the effects of the crisis. If the current trajectory is not reversed, Asia and the Pacific will suffer more than most other regions from the impacts of climate change, air pollution, and biodiversity loss.

Coal and other fossil fuels have had a major role in providing access to energy in Asia and the Pacific and enabling the region's economic development. Continued utilization of fossil fuels, however, is detrimental to the environment and hastens climate change. In 2019, about 50% of global carbon dioxide (CO_2) emissions from fossil fuel (coal, oil, and natural gas) combustion came from Asia and the Pacific. The combustion of fossil fuels is also the main source of local air pollutants that cause immediate and lasting harm to public health and ecosystem services. Some of the most polluted cities in the world in terms of annual average particulate concentration are in Asia and the Pacific. Consequently, the energy sector of Asia and the Pacific is a critical area for a direct and effective response to climate change, and for building climate and disaster resilience. ADB's deep and long engagement in this sector means that it is uniquely placed to play a pivotal role.

The region's energy intensity remains higher than the global average, and the potential for the application of energy efficiency measures is large. There is a need to accelerate progress on energy efficiency gains across the region, which can contribute to the agendas of energy security and energy access while also producing cost and environmental benefits.

Climate change contributes to the increase in the frequency and intensity of extreme weather events and associated risks. Many DMCs are highly exposed and vulnerable to resulting natural hazards such as sea level rise, changes in rainfall patterns, cyclones, floods, landslides, droughts, and heat waves. Pacific countries and other small island states, as well as some areas in South Asia, are the first

[8] ADB. 2017. *Climate Change Operational Framework 2017–2030: Enhanced Action for Low Greenhouse-Gas Emissions and Climate-Resilient Development.* Manila.

to encounter the impacts of rising sea levels because of warming trends. DMCs are suffering losses from disasters because of insufficient regard for climate and disaster risk in the design and location of infrastructure. The impact of climate change and the disruption of ecosystems can severely impair livelihoods and food security, which in turn can undermine human health.

This makes the proper siting and design of clean energy projects critical in minimizing land use conflicts and preserving natural and cultural values, such as scenic landscapes and biologically productive ecosystems. Upholding the ecological integrity of ecosystems increases the resilience of these ecosystems, as well as the socioeconomic systems and community health they support.

Similarly, it is important to consider the environmental impact of the disposal of clean energy equipment such as solar panels, wind turbine blades, and batteries at the end of their useful life when designing clean energy projects and related procurement systems. DMCs need to be provided with support to put in place proper disposal mechanisms and to bear related costs.

To enhance disaster resilience in the energy sector, many advanced economies in the region developed high levels of grid redundancy, for example, or shifted from overhead lines to underground cabling. Such measures are costly and may seem unaffordable for DMCs whose priorities are to extend service to unserved areas or strengthen the grid to tackle serious service deficits. However, not investing in resilience measures can lead to higher life cycle costs because of infrastructure failure and rebuilding needs after extreme events. Resilience is the ability to withstand extreme events and recover quickly. Resilient infrastructure does not only pertain to robustness and durability of physical assets. It is also about infrastructure that buffers society from shocks and crises. Resilience is about having an "inclusive infrastructure that helps the most vulnerable segments of society withstand the shockwaves."[9] Thus, ADB is committed to disassociate the region's energy sector from environmental degradation that puts its DMCs' development at risk.

4. Sector Governance

Most of the region's electricity market systems and their supporting regulations were developed based on a traditional, centralized system not designed to deal with the supply-side variability that comes from intermittent renewable sources. Today, they are facing the increasing challenges of accommodating a large role of renewable energy, the deployment of distributed energy resources, and demand-side participation in the operation of the power system. The region's governments continue to deregulate and reform their power subsectors to increase efficiency and restructure state-owned utilities to allow competition. New power exchanges are likely to emerge, and existing ones are likely to be strengthened. Newer power generation technologies and fuels are being placed on a more than equal footing with fossil fuels, particularly by pricing the social and environmental costs of fossil fuel use through mechanisms such as carbon taxes, emission-trading systems, and international offset mechanisms. However, cost-reflective tariffs and governance measures to ensure sector accountability and sustainability remain an issue in many countries in the region. Accommodating greater flexibility and new technologies will require governance, market, and DMC regulatory reforms.

---

[9]   M. Aizawa. 2020. *The Values of Inclusive Infrastructure in a Post-coronavirus World.* International Institute for Sustainable Development.

Subsidies have long been used in the energy sector to promote desired objectives. They have been used traditionally to ensure the affordability of energy services, and transport fuels were subsidized to ensure economic productivity, mobility, and quality of life. More recently, subsidies have been used to accelerate the deployment of renewable energy. Fossil fuel subsidies are typically concentrated in upstream wholesale energy production and distribution operations such as coal mining and petroleum fuel supply, while renewable energy subsidies are typically concentrated at the project and retail end of the supply chain, such as rooftop solar. Financial incentives in the form of feed-in tariffs for renewable energy are now being eliminated or reduced as renewable energy has become more competitive. To avoid unwanted market distortions and promote economic efficiency, energy subsidies should be targeted, timebound, and transparent across the full spectrum of fuel types and energy services. Targeting subsidies to achieve their objectives without unintended consequences remains an important policy challenge in the region.

As the Asia and Pacific region recovers from COVID-19, improving the resilience and security of the energy sector has been clearly identified as a priority. Institutional capacity building remains an important factor in achieving good governance. Although most, but not all, energy systems have operated well so far, their typical reliance on imported expertise, technologies, and fossil fuels makes them vulnerable. Renewable energy technologies, when manufactured, deployed, and maintained locally, have the potential to create a resilient energy generation source that uses indigenous resources. While COVID-19 has initially reduced the cost of imported fossil fuels because of lower demand, the recent crisis has exposed DMCs to the risks of access to and price volatility of fossil fuels. Therefore, a reduction in the use of imported fuel augments the potential resilience of the energy systems of DMCs. Moreover, the increased use of information and communication technologies in energy infrastructure will require a focus on cybersecurity to avoid security threats.

Given the scale of investment requirements of about $800 billion per year, energy reforms in DMCs should lead to more opportunities for private sector participation, particularly in the subsector of electricity generation.[10] While a fully open subsector with a competitive electricity market is still a rarity in the region, many DMCs have enabled private sector investments via regulated entry points such as public–private partnerships (PPPs), renewable energy auctions, and independent power producers with long-term power purchase agreements. ADB will continue to work to mobilize higher levels of concessional financing and private sector investments; increase technical support; and focus on catalytic activities, innovations, and affordable transfer of green technologies.

D. The Changing Energy Landscape and Opportunities

There have been many, and fundamental changes in the energy landscape in the past decade, notably the global commitment to universal energy access and climate change, and the rapid development in low-carbon technologies. In the same decade, there have been significant advances in economic development and energy modernization in Asia and the Pacific. Consolidating achievements, addressing emerging challenges and opportunities, and ensuring a just and equitable transition to

---

[10] ADB. 2017. *Meeting Asia's Infrastructure Needs*. Manila.

a low-carbon future in Asia and the Pacific will require ADB's continued support for its DMCs on a broad range of energy issues.

1.   The Dynamic and Evolving Cost of Renewable Energy

The transition to cleaner and more sustainable energy systems has begun, and significant declines in the costs of renewable energy technologies are accelerating this transition. Between 2010 and 2019, the costs of solar photovoltaic (PV) systems decreased by 82%, while those of concentrating solar power plants fell by 47%, followed by onshore (39%) and offshore (29%) wind farms.[11] These trends—which are projected to continue—have led to a reduction in the cost differential between traditional fossil fuel power generation technologies and renewable energy generators. The cost of electricity from unsubsidized renewable energy can be lower than that from new conventional generators, and, in some cases, renewable power costs are competitive with those of existing conventional generators.[12] The development of ultra-high-voltage technology for both alternating and direct current electricity transmission, together with rapidly declining costs for solar and wind power, have increased the feasibility of large-scale development and the use of hydropower, wind, and solar resources in remote, subregional, and inter-subregional contexts.

However, the intermittent nature of solar and wind energy sources also means that grid-scale storage and alternative generation capacity are required to integrate them effectively. Such complete systems needed to provide energy services equivalent to those from conventional energy sources add to the cost of effective deployment of renewable energy. Also, it is important to note that the impact of the COVID-19 pandemic and the recent solar PV supply chains issues have resulted in escalation of the price of renewable energy technologies. These factors will slow down the growth of renewable energy deployment, which needs to be overcome with appropriate timely support from ADB, particularly in smaller DMCs.

2.   Emerging Low-Carbon Technologies

In addition to cost declines for established technologies, newer technologies are maturing that can contribute to a clean energy transition. Battery energy storage systems have experienced cost reductions and performance improvements, amplifying their relevance in managing variable renewable generation. Electrification; carbon capture, use, and storage (CCUS); green ammonia and hydrogen (made without fossil fuels); and advanced biofuels can all play a role in transitioning the business areas that are more difficult to decarbonize, such as long-range transport, industry, and space cooling and heating. Battery electric vehicles, plug-in hybrid technologies, and fuel cell systems enable the transport sector to move away from fossil fuels. In industries, direct electric heating, electric arcs, and induction heating offer opportunities to electrify processes that require high temperatures. Heat pumps can provide efficient heating for industries as well as space heating and cooling, even in a context of generation sources with low heat content. ADB will facilitate and support DMCs in deploying these new low-carbon technologies and solutions and technology transfer, as appropriate.

---

[11]   International Renewable Energy Agency (IRENA). 2020. *Renewable Power Generation Costs in 2019*. Abu Dhabi.

[12]   Lazard. 2020. *Levelized Cost of Energy and Levelized Cost of Storage—2020*.

3. *Maturing Digital and Smart Technologies*

Parallel to the rapid development of renewable energy technology, digital and smart technologies have been rapidly developed and are maturing. Digitalization has an important role in energy transition because it enables and facilitates decarbonization and decentralization. Digital and smart technologies are transforming the energy industry in a lot of ways—from helping integrate variable renewable energy sources, stabilizing the grid, and reducing technical and commercial losses. The surge in the advances in digitalization, however, comes not without trade-offs as this can also increase the energy sector's exposure to operational risks, particularly cybersecurity and information technology supply chain risks.

Blockchain can support decentralized energy transactions, metering and billing; artificial intelligence can enhance forecasting and provide new insights into large operational asset dataset; mobile connectivity and tablet devices can standardize field-based workflow and automate data collection; drones and remote sensing can enhance safety of wind turbines, solar farms, and T&D lines; big data and data management can benchmark and analyze asset performance; and business platforms can share data between asset owners, operators, regulators, and investors. Today, digitalization enables large-scale data collection, information processing, and decision-making—helping achieve much higher system visibility and controllability, and thus improved decision-making and control outcomes, making the grid more reliable, flexible, and resilient.

4. *Unfinished Development Agenda in the Region*

ADB's Strategy 2030 notes that "Asia and the Pacific has made great strides in poverty reduction and economic growth in the last 50 years." Long-term continuous economic growth has been observed in many parts of the region including the People's Republic of China, Southeast Asia, and South Asia. In the last 10 years, there has been significant progress in electrification, and power systems have been modernized in many DMCs in the region.

The development agenda in the region, however, persists, as poverty, rising inequality, the growing threat of climate change and environmental risks, and large infrastructure gaps remain to be addressed to achieve the goals set under the SDGs and the Paris Agreement.

E. Energy Policy 2021 and the Energy Sector Directional Guide

The Energy Policy 2021 was approved by the ADB Board in October 2021, to support universal access to reliable, sustainable, and affordable energy services, while promoting low-carbon transition in Asia and the Pacific.[13] Aligned with Strategy 2030, the Energy Policy 2021 will guide the energy sector support to the region as it responds to the challenges both in terms of energy access and security, and climate change and environmental sustainability.

---

[13] ADB. 2021. *Energy Policy: Supporting Low-Carbon Transition in Asia and the Pacific.* Manila.

Consistent with ADB's Strategy 2030, the SDGs, and the Paris Agreement, the Energy Policy 2021 adopts a common but differentiated approach in supporting DMCs' commitments to SDGs and nationally determined contributions (NDCs). ADB will prioritize essential energy access in the poorest and most vulnerable countries through greater use of low-carbon and renewable energy sources and rehabilitate infrastructure to enhance energy security and climate resilience. In low-income and lower-middle-income countries, ADB will continue to support reforms in the energy sector, including reforms of state-owned enterprises; the development of green and inclusive energy infrastructure to enhance productivity and competitiveness; the promotion of gender equality; and greater participation of the private sector in delivering energy infrastructure and services.

Formally closing the door on coal financing, the Energy Policy 2021 supports the phase-out of coal and a just transition in the region. Recognizing the massive demand for investment in the region, the new policy prioritizes ADB's resources to leverage commercial financing where possible, to tackle the most difficult energy challenges.

This ESDG, which has been developed in parallel with directional guides of a few other sectors, such as transport, water, and urban, assesses the current and future energy sector trends, challenges, and opportunities, and how ADB can best position itself to add value in energy sector operations. It aims to support ADB staff in conducting energy sector operations in line with the Energy Policy 2021 up to 2030. The guide also outlines the priorities and focus for the energy sector in line with ADB's Strategy 2030.

The directional guide is a living document and will be updated as needed. A midterm review is to be conducted following the expected review of the Energy Policy in 2025.

II WHERE WE WANT TO BE

A. ADB's Strategy 2030 and Operational Priorities

ADB approved its corporate strategy, Strategy 2030: Achieving a Prosperous, Inclusive, Resilient, and Sustainable Asia and the Pacific in 2018. Strategy 2030 sets out what ADB should do and why and establishes seven OPs for the delivery of the strategy. For each of the seven OPs, operational plans have been prepared:[14]

OP1 Addressing remaining poverty and reducing inequalities. Human development and social inclusion, quality jobs, education and training, better health, social protection.

OP2 Accelerating progress in gender equality. Scaled-up support for gender equality; women's economic empowerment; gender equality in human development, decision-making, and leadership; reducing time poverty for women; strengthening women's resilience to shocks.

OP 3 Tackling climate change, building climate and disaster resilience. Enhancing environmental sustainability low GHG emissions development, approach to building climate and disaster resilience, environmental sustainability, water–food–energy security nexus.

OP 4 Making cities more livable. Integrated solutions, funding for cities, inclusive and participatory urban planning, climate resilience and disaster management.

OP 5 Promoting rural development and food security. Market connectivity and agricultural value chain linkages, agricultural productivity and food security, food safety.

OP 6 Strengthening governance and institutional capacity. Public management reforms and financial sustainability, service delivery, capacity, and standards.

OP 7 Fostering regional cooperation and integration. Greater and higher quality connectivity expanded trade and investment and increased and diversified regional public goods.

Energy is central to inclusive socioeconomic development and plays a key role in each of the seven OPs and thus in the delivery of Strategy 2030. Figure 4 shows how the energy sector contributes to the seven OPs of Strategy 2030.

---

[14] These include (i) ADB. 2019. *Strategy 2030 Operational Priority 1: Addressing Remaining Poverty and Reducing Inequalities, 2019–2024*. Manila; (ii) ADB. 2019. *Strategy 2030 Operational Priority 2: Accelerating Progress in Gender Equality, 2019–2024*. Manila; (iii) ADB. 2019. *Strategy 2030 Operational Priority 3: Tackling Climate Change, Building Climate and Disaster Resilience, and Enhancing Environmental Sustainability, 2019–2024*. Manila; (iv) ADB. 2019. *Strategy 2030 Operational Priority 4: Making Cities More Livable, 2019–2024*. Manila; (v) ADB. 2019. *Strategy 2030 Operational Priority 5: Promoting Rural Development and Food Security, 2019–2024*. Manila; (vi) ADB. 2019. *Strategy 2030 Operational Priority 6: Strengthening Governance and Institutional Capacity, 2019–2024*. Manila; and (vii) ADB. 2019. *Strategy 2030 Operational Priority 7: Fostering Regional Cooperation and Integration, 2019–2024*. Manila. An overview document was also prepared, which brought together the main points of these operational plans. See ADB. 2019. *Strategy 2030 Operational Plans Overview*. Manila.

Figure 4: Energy Sector Contributions to Strategy 2030 Operational Priorities

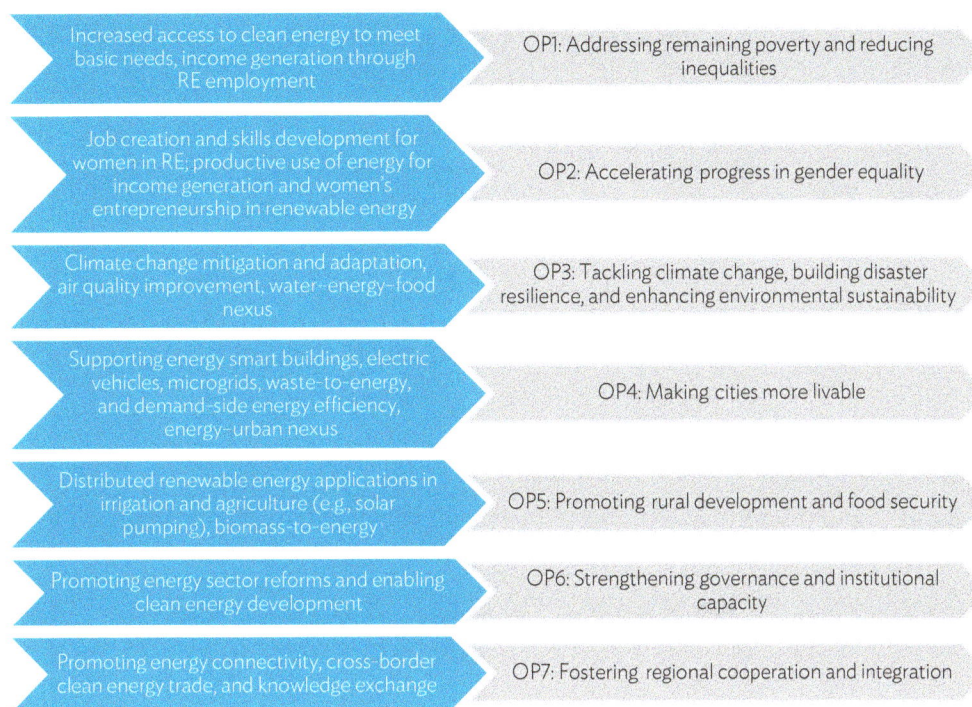

Energy Sector Contribution	Operational Priority
Increased access to clean energy to meet basic needs, income generation through RE employment	OP1: Addressing remaining poverty and reducing inequalities
Job creation and skills development for women in RE; productive use of energy for income generation and women's entrepreneurship in renewable energy	OP2: Accelerating progress in gender equality
Climate change mitigation and adaptation, air quality improvement, water–energy–food nexus	OP3: Tackling climate change, building disaster resilience, and enhancing environmental sustainability
Supporting energy smart buildings, electric vehicles, microgrids, waste-to-energy, and demand-side energy efficiency, energy–urban nexus	OP4: Making cities more livable
Distributed renewable energy applications in irrigation and agriculture (e.g., solar pumping), biomass-to-energy	OP5: Promoting rural development and food security
Promoting energy sector reforms and enabling clean energy development	OP6: Strengthening governance and institutional capacity
Promoting energy connectivity, cross-border clean energy trade, and knowledge exchange	OP7: Fostering regional cooperation and integration

OP = operational priority, RE = renewable energy.
Source: Asian Development Bank (formerly Sustainable Development and Climate Change Department).

B. Sustainable Development Goals and the Paris Agreement

The United Nations' "SDGs are the blueprint to achieve a better and more sustainable future for all" in addressing the challenges besetting the world such as poverty, inequality, climate change, environmental degradation, peace, and justice. SDG7—Universal Energy Access by 2030 puts the energy sector front and center to "ensure access to affordable, reliable, sustainable and modern energy for all."[15]

In 2015, at the 21st session of the Conference of the Parties (COP 21), the Paris Agreement was adopted uniting all nations to combat climate change with enhanced support to assist developing countries. The Paris Agreement requires all countries to put forward their best efforts in confronting climate change through their respective NDCs. Since then, many countries have committed to ambitious long-term plans and the number of countries announcing net-zero emissions targets by the middle of the 21st century has increased.

In October 2021, ADB announced the increase its climate finance target to $100 billion for 2019–2030 from the $80 billion announced in 2015 to help its DMCs fight climate change.

---

[15]   United Nations. *Take Action for the Sustainable Development Goals.*

Climate financing will support mitigation and adaptation projects, ADB's private sector operations, a green COVID-19 recovery, and sector reforms in DMCs.

ADB is aligning its operations with the goals of the Paris Agreement by supporting the development and rollout of climate action plans by its DMCs. ADB will align its financing with the mitigation and adaptation goals of the Paris Agreement, for 100% of sovereign operations and 85% of nonsovereign operations by July 2023, and 100% of nonsovereign operations by July 2025.

ADB supports DMCs' commitments to the SDGs and the Paris Agreement. The objectives of ADB's energy sector operations are to help DMCs accelerate the development of sustainable and resilient energy systems that provide reliable and affordable access for all, foster inclusive economic growth and social development, and support the low-carbon transition in Asia and the Pacific.

C. Future Assistance Focus

Recognizing the massive financing needs in the energy sector across the region, ADB's resources must be prioritized to tackle the most demanding energy challenges. ADB's assistance will focus on meeting the emerging needs and add value to the clients in the region. To support the low-carbon transition, and based on the emerging needs in the region, the areas of delivery will focus on the "4Ds"— decarbonization, decreasing energy intensity, digitalization, and decentralization.

1. Decarbonization

Asia and the Pacific is the battlefield of climate change and urgent actions on decarbonization are needed. ADB will facilitate the low-carbon transition by assisting DMCs in (i) accelerating the deployment of renewable energy, (ii) pursuing strategic decarbonization and the phase-out of coal while ensuring a just transition, and (iii) developing policies and regulations to support low-carbon technologies and introducing market-based instruments, including carbon pricing.

ADB will cease financing new coal-fired power and heating plants, support DMCs in achieving a planned phase-out of coal in the Asia and Pacific region, and foster a just transition that considers its impacts on people and communities. ADB will support clean and sustainable energy solutions, such as supply and demand-side energy efficiency, renewable energy, distributed renewable energy generation, electric mobility, as well as emerging low-carbon technologies such as CCUS, biofuels, and green hydrogen. ADB will also support associated infrastructure such as smart and resilient power grids and battery energy storage systems to ensure the integration of an increasing share of renewable energy sources. ADB will help DMCs in strengthening the quality and capacity of energy sector institutions to undertake policy reforms. The reforms should lead to measurable improvements in the security, quality, affordability, resilience, and environmental sustainability of energy supply.

ADB will vigorously pursue an Energy Transition Mechanism (ETM) to accelerate decommissioning of existing coal power plants and replace them with renewable energy sources accompanied by ancillary services to provide the same energy services. ETM may be adopted to suit specific country requirements so that it can be expanded to cover major coal power-dominated economies in the Asia and Pacific region.

Transition technologies will be utilized to reduce carbon dioxide (CO_2) intensity, such as improving efficiency of existing fossil fuel-based energy facilities and switching from coal to natural gas. While natural gas is a fossil fuel, it is 50%–60% less carbon-intensive than coal and can be used to stabilize the variability of solar and wind power. The 2021 Energy Policy sets the conditions for using natural gas that all ADB-financed projects must comply with.

ADB recognizes that natural gas has a role to play as a transitional fuel that can support power system flexibility under specific circumstances. ADB may also support projects that improve universal access to modern and clean energy for electricity and cooking for those without access. ADB may finance investments in natural gas infrastructure—including gas T&D pipelines, liquefied natural gas (LNG) terminals, and storage facilities—and natural gas-based end-use facilities. However, gas projects are subject to a set of screening criteria consistent with the Paris Agreement.

All projects involving natural gas must meet all of the following conditions: (i) no other low-carbon or zero-carbon technology, or combination thereof, can provide the same service at an equivalent or lower cost at a comparable scale; (ii) the project's operating lifetime is consistent with the carbon stabilization trajectory aiming to achieve carbon neutrality by about 2050, and by a time set by DMCs that is consistent with their NDCs, and the project also avoids long-term lock-in into carbon infrastructure and the associated risk of creating stranded assets; and (iii) the project is economically viable considering the social cost of carbon and an operating lifetime consistent with condition (ii). Additional requirements are specified in the Energy Policy 2021 depending on the type of natural gas project.

ADB recognizes the role of nuclear energy in the decarbonization pathway given its ability to replace energy services from fossil fuel fired base-load power plants. Therefore, ADB will include nuclear analysis in the development of long-term energy plans and climate strategies, as appropriate. However, ADB will not finance investments in nuclear energy given complexities associated with such investments including issues related to nuclear proliferation, waste management, and safety.

2. *Decreasing Energy Intensity*

Improving energy efficiency, thereby reducing energy intensity is an effective step toward the peaking of greenhouse gas emissions and carbon neutrality. ADB will support developing member countries in increasing energy efficiency investments to improve energy intensity and energy productivity. ADB will support demand-side energy efficiency planning and promote minimum energy performance standards for appliances and equipment, fuel economy standards for vehicles, standards for electric motors in industry, mandatory energy audits, and energy management policies for large industrial and commercial companies and building codes. ADB will promote these demand-side energy efficiency measures in new and existing public buildings at both national and local levels, combining it with rooftop solar and electric vehicle charging investments. ADB will also help mainstream energy efficiency investments through financial intermediation loans and grants involving commercial banks and other financial institutions.

ADB will promote increased demand-side energy efficiency through policy support, use of innovative financing instruments, and mobilization of private sector resources. It will provide DMCs with technical assistance, grants, and loans to establish legal and regulatory frameworks, policies, and programs that support energy efficiency; and develop incentive mechanisms for consumers, utilities, energy service companies, and other market players. ADB may combine financing with capacity building and technical assistance to help consolidate scattered industrial, commercial, and residential opportunities, and induce behavioral changes for energy conservation.

T&D losses and inefficiencies remain a significant problem in many DMCs. ADB will promote increased efficiency in T&D networks. ADB will keep supporting DMCs' efforts to increase supply-side energy efficiency by building on its experience in reducing losses in electricity T&D. This includes using the latest technologies, such as high-temperature, low-sag conductors that can withstand higher operating temperatures and carry more power than conventional conductors, and dynamic line rating to help maximize load. ADB also supports the use of drones with advanced sensors for inspection and maintenance of transmission lines to identify and mitigate any risks to the power distribution network and enhance the safety of maintenance staff. Moreover, ADB will support the use of digital technologies such as smart meters to support demand-side energy efficiency.

3. *Digitalization*

Digitalization is transforming the energy industry and is an enabler of decarbonization and decentralization. Digitalization and smart technologies are important in the low-carbon transition by enabling renewable energy integration and enhancing system flexibility, reliability, and resilience.

ADB will assist DMCs in improving the reliability of electricity supply, connecting additional supply capacity to the grid, reducing technical losses and power theft, and reaching outlying and previously unserved regions. ADB will help deploy digital technologies such as smart meters to reduce technical and commercial losses and encourage demand-side energy efficiency, peer-to-peer trading using blockchain technology for energy markets, and artificial intelligence for predictive grid management and grid resilience. ADB may also support the use of advanced conductors, dynamic line rating, advanced grid control systems such as anti-blackout technology, various demand–response mechanisms, on-grid electricity storage, distributed generation, cybersecurity, and digital smart grid solutions, which are among the available options to improve power system operations management assisted by increased grid reliability, flexibility, and resilience.

4. *Decentralization*

Today, power systems are being decentralized, thanks to renewable energy and advanced technologies. Decentralized energy systems can support energy access, improve operation efficiency, and reduce greenhouse gas emissions and other environmental impacts. The trend forms part of the low-carbon transition and DMCs need support on technology transfer and market reforms to accommodate decentralization.

ADB will support low-carbon, decentralized technologies such as distributed generations, renewable energy-based micro and mini-grids, home systems, and energy storage systems. ADB will also support increased competition and private sector participation in DMCs' energy markets to contribute greater dynamism to the energy sector and take advantage of opportunities created by new technologies and business models.

ADB will support the next generation of electricity market reforms, focused on open access to transmission systems and retail competition. It will help in the unbundling of vertically integrated utilities, the corporatization of specific utility functions, securitization, asset recycling, and—if requested—the privatization of public enterprises created in the process.

D. Theory of Change

The energy sector vision embodied in this ESDG is captured in the theory of change in Figure 5. The expected impact is supporting ADB's DMCs "to achieve the vision of an inclusive low-carbon transition in Asia and the Pacific." This will require ADB to collaborate with various stakeholders working in the energy sector and aligning its inputs to support its DMCs to achieve the goal.

ADB's support will focus on five key, intermediate outcomes: (i) universal energy access including clean cooking, heating, and cooling; (ii) communities with improved climate and disaster resilience;

Figure 5: Theory of Change of the Energy Sector Directional Guide

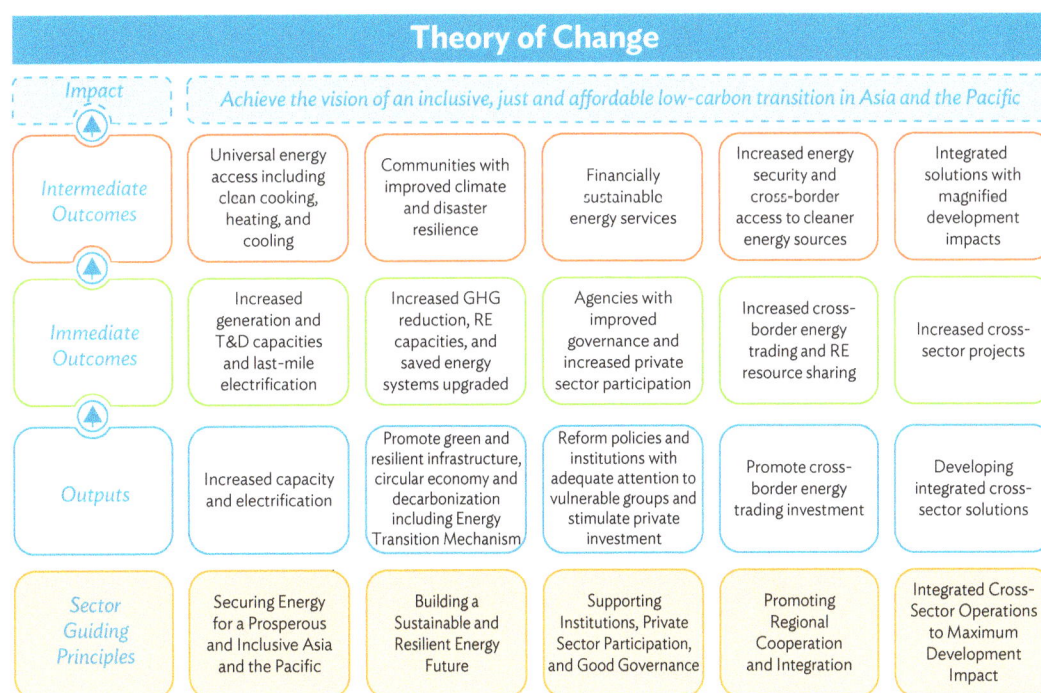

Theory of Change

Impact	Achieve the vision of an inclusive, just and affordable low-carbon transition in Asia and the Pacific				
Intermediate Outcomes	Universal energy access including clean cooking, heating, and cooling	Communities with improved climate and disaster resilience	Financially sustainable energy services	Increased energy security and cross-border access to cleaner energy sources	Integrated solutions with magnified development impacts
Immediate Outcomes	Increased generation and T&D capacities and last-mile electrification	Increased GHG reduction, RE capacities, and saved energy systems upgraded	Agencies with improved governance and increased private sector participation	Increased cross-border energy trading and RE resource sharing	Increased cross-sector projects
Outputs	Increased capacity and electrification	Promote green and resilient infrastructure, circular economy and decarbonization including Energy Transition Mechanism	Reform policies and institutions with adequate attention to vulnerable groups and stimulate private investment	Promote cross-border energy trading investment	Developing integrated cross-sector solutions
Sector Guiding Principles	Securing Energy for a Prosperous and Inclusive Asia and the Pacific	Building a Sustainable and Resilient Energy Future	Supporting Institutions, Private Sector Participation, and Good Governance	Promoting Regional Cooperation and Integration	Integrated Cross-Sector Operations to Maximum Development Impact

GHG = greenhouse gas, RE = renewable energy, T&D = transmission and distribution.

Note: The Energy Policy 2021 is based on five policy principles, which are also the guiding principles of this Energy Sector Directional Guide as depicted in the chart.

Source: Asian Development Bank (formerly Sustainable Development and Climate Change Department).

(iii) financially sustainable energy services; (iv) increased energy security and cross-border access to cleaner energy sources; and (v) integrated solutions with magnified development impacts.

There are five key outputs that ADB will support in assisting its DMCs to achieve the outcomes. The first output will focus on increased generation capacity and electrification by supporting last-mile electrification and T&D development. The second output is to promote green and resilient infrastructure, circular economy, and reduced emissions by supporting a planned phase-out of coal, promoting energy efficiency, low-carbon technologies and strengthening energy infrastructure to integrate renewable energy while curtailing environmental degradation. The third output will focus on reform policies and institutions, and stimulate private investment by supporting sector reforms, institution strengthening, and private sector participation through policy dialogues and technical assistance. The fourth output is to promote cross-border energy trading investment by supporting regional and subregional cooperation and the development of cross-border markets and infrastructure. The fifth output will focus on developing integrated cross-sector solutions through combined finance, knowledge, partnerships, and country-focused approach.

ADB will focus on improving the quality of its inputs including technical assistance, grants, and loans provided during the design and implementation of the projects and programs through knowledge, partnerships, and innovation. Knowledge will inform project development and design to generate the best of outcomes. Partnerships in both cofinancing and knowledge will better leverage energy projects. And innovation will drive cutting-edge and effective interventions in the sector.

E. Overarching Considerations

The primary objective of the energy sector operations is to help DMCs provide universal access to reliable and affordable clean and sustainable energy, while accelerating a just, low-carbon transition that prioritizes ecologically friendly technologies. The ensuing paragraphs summarize the overarching considerations for energy operations.

1. Multidimensional Support

The Energy Policy 2021 underscores that ADB's support to developing member countries in the energy sector requires ongoing commitment to Sustainable Development Goal 7 and encourages urgent action to combat climate change and its impacts and protect environments while fostering economic growth. ADB recognizes that energy services must be affordable, reliable, and resilient for productive uses, urban populations, and rural communities. It realizes that these objectives cannot be achieved by only supporting infrastructure investments through technical assistance, grants, guarantees and other risk management instruments, and loans. Such objectives also require robust long-term planning, accelerated deployment and transfers of sustainable green technologies, improved governance, favorable policy environments, more efficient institutions, and better service delivery by public and private operators. Hence, ADB will continue to support institutional development, policy reforms, and regional energy cooperation through integrated approaches with knowledge sharing, technical advice, capacity building, and financing, consistent with the G20 Principles for Quality Infrastructure Investment to enhance efficiency, affordability, sustainability, and resilience of new energy assets.

2. *Differentiated Approach*

In accordance with Strategy 2030, and in recognition of the significant diversity across developing member countries, the implementation of the energy sector framework will adopt common but differentiated approaches in line with each developing member country's level of economic development, resource endowment, and nationally determined low-carbon transition pathways. ADB will prioritize support for essential energy access services in the poorest and most vulnerable countries, including fragile and conflict-affected situations and small island developing states, through greater use of low-carbon and renewable energy sources, and assistance for the rehabilitation of infrastructure to enhance energy security and climate resilience. Support for a just transition will also factor in resource considerations in line with this differentiated approach. In low-income and lower-middle-income countries, ADB will continue to support reforms in the energy sector, including reforms of state-owned enterprises; the development of green and inclusive energy infrastructure to enhance productivity and competitiveness; the promotion of gender equality; and greater participation of the private sector in delivering energy infrastructure and services.

ADB supports the principle of common but differentiated responsibilities and respective capabilities considering national circumstances that is embedded in the Paris Agreement. It allows countries to reflect their unique circumstances and provides them with the necessary flexibility in the choice of their measures as they plan to achieve global peaking of GHG emissions and carbon neutrality as soon as possible. The Parties to the Paris Agreement have agreed to reflect their highest possible ambition in establishing their low-carbon pathways, recognizing that it will take longer for developing countries to reach their peak in GHG emissions. ADB will therefore support all DMCs through finance, technical assistance, policy dialogue, and knowledge sharing to increase the ambition of their national energy plans, NDCs, and long-term climate strategies; and will encourage the low-carbon transition in the region by all means available and appropriate to national circumstances.

3. *Inclusive Energy Operations*

ADB will conduct its energy sector activities in line with the principles of justice, equity, diversity, and inclusiveness. In accordance with Strategy 2030's operational priority 2 (OP2), gender equality and women's increased leadership in the public and private sectors are recognized as valuable goals in their own right, as well as for their value in helping advance socioeconomic development. Despite progress in Asia and the Pacific, persistent gender gaps remain. Gender equality in employment, decision-making, and leadership will therefore continue to be an important goal throughout the consultation, planning, and implementation of energy sector operations.

ADB recognizes its duty to inform and engage with local populations during the planning of renewable energy and infrastructure resilience projects that will affect their lives. This process will seek to empower communities through meaningful consultation. It is essential that the potential benefits for and impacts on all disadvantaged and vulnerable groups—women, the poor, racial and ethnic minorities, indigenous peoples, people with disabilities, older persons, and other marginalized people—are carefully considered during project or program preparation and implementation. Project teams should conduct meaningful consultation with care and with an understanding of the overlapping nature of issues faced by many disadvantaged and vulnerable groups.

ADB will promote inclusivity by facilitating stakeholder participation in the formulation of policies and the design, implementation, and monitoring of energy projects. Relevant stakeholders for ensuring country-level energy policies, projects, and programs are developed within the principle of inclusive energy operations include academia, think tanks and research institutions, civil society organizations, community-based organizations, and philanthropic foundations.

Energy sector processes will have a key role in determining the future impacts of climate change. Long-term changes—such as air pollution, the disruption of ecosystems, rising sea levels, and changes to rainfall patterns—will have the greatest impact on the future lives of today's children. It is therefore incumbent on ADB to ensure that children and youth also have a voice in the energy sector processes that will determine their future, and that those views are given due weight in the consultation procedures during preparation and implementation of energy projects.[16]

4. *Concessional Climate Resources*

ADB aims to become the Climate Bank of Asia and the Pacific by playing a leading role with developing member countries and key partners to deploy new and innovative investments, knowledge, and strategies. The ongoing energy transformation is causing a surge in the need for energy investments in Asia and the Pacific—on top of the already high demand for infrastructure investment driven by urbanization, industrialization, and population growth. ADB will use its competitive advantage, convening power, and regional knowledge to leverage international climate finance, including international concessional resources, to help its DMCs achieve their national targets and international commitments expeditiously and to achieve a rapid shift to greener and cleaner economies. ADB will also continue to work to mobilize higher levels of concessional financing and private sector investments to support the necessary transition.

5. *Expanding Private Sector Participation*

An ADB strategic and operational priority is to ensure an expanded role for private sector financing and solutions to complement what is provided by ADB's sovereign operations. The private sector not only hinges on the extensive resources of private capital but also on the private sector spearheading innovation in technology and business models that support creativity, dynamism, and efficiency in the pursuit of sustainable solutions. ADB will use private sector operations and PPP resources (the Private Sector Operations Department [PSOD] and the Office of Markets Development and Public–Private Partnership [OMDP]) in close collaboration with its public sector operations to provide integrated solutions to DMCs in the energy sector. Public sector operations, including project lending, policy-based lending, and technical assistance, can advance energy sector reforms and regulatory frameworks that allow the private sector to make an important contribution to the energy transition.

While private financing has been active in the power generation subsector, it is vital to take the One ADB approach, for the energy sector operations to work closely with PSOD and the transaction advisory services of the OMDP, to achieve better outcomes.

---

[16] United Nations. 1989. *Convention on the Rights of the Child*, Treaty no. 27531. United Nations Treaty Series, 1577. Article 12.2; ADB. 2021. *A Sourcebook for Engaging with CSOs in ADB Operations*. Manila.

ADB can increase project viability through project financing, PPPs, technical assistance, blended finance with concessional funds, and other instruments that bring in private sector capital from the market. Such interventions can be supplemented, and their impact enhanced by mobilizing third-party concessional financing facilities that can be deployed taking advantage of ADB's operational and sector expertise. ADB will also help structure sustainable energy projects to ensure optimal risk sharing, and provide risk management services through guarantees, interest rate hedging instruments, and other products such as credit insurance. Financial risk management instruments can bring comfort to and engage the commercial finance sector in early-stage markets and can be key to achieving investments in first-of-a-kind projects.

ADB will seek to increase the volume of financing through its PSOD for energy projects that are aligned with the Energy Policy 2021, while at the same time recognizing the need to avoid crowding out other sources of private sector financing and steering investment resources away from countries with less-developed financial markets. Hence, ADB will guide its nonsovereign energy operations to expand into new markets, including challenging markets such as fragile and conflict-affected situations and small island developing states. In this context, ADB will consider smaller project sizes with potentially higher risk and development impact, including inclusive business models to achieve greater gender equality, job creation, and access to affordable clean energy for households and the productive use of energy.

6. *Accounting for Externalities*

ADB incorporates the social cost of carbon across all operations including in the energy sector. The current unit value used by ADB ($46.1/ton of CO_2 equivalent in 2021) is based on the empirical estimates of the global social cost of carbon reported in the Fifth Assessment Report by the Intergovernmental Panel on Climate Change. This is to be increased by 2% annually in real terms to allow for the potentially increasing marginal damage of global warming over time. This unit value is used in economic analyses to estimate the value of avoided GHG emissions for projects that reduce emissions and the cost in damage created for projects that increase emissions. The unit value will be revised in the future as more and newer estimates of damage caused by climate change become available.

F. Guiding Principles of the Energy Policy 2021

The Energy Policy 2021 is based on five policy principles, which are also the foundations of the ESDG.

Principle 1: Securing Energy for a Prosperous and Inclusive Asia and the Pacific

The first policy principle obligates ADB to work toward securing energy for a prosperous and inclusive Asia and the Pacific by promoting distribution networks that increase access to power, light, clean cooking and drinking water, sanitation and health, and clean heating and cooling. This principle is aligned with the objective of OP1 to address remaining poverty and reduce inequalities. Ensuring access to modern forms of energy improves well-being and creates opportunities for productive activities, including employment and businesses for those living in rural settings and informal settlements. Modern energy access also contributes to reducing persistent gender gaps, gender inequality, and women's burden of care and unpaid work, as called for in OP2. ADB will promote energy access through various approaches, including extension of distribution grids, renewable energy-based microgrids and home systems, clean cooking, heating, and cooling. ADB will support electric mobility to help make cities more livable by improving ambient air quality, as called for in OP3 and OP4. Renewable energy development contributes to rural development, particularly through off-grid electrification programs and through wider access to clean energy as per SDG7, and contributes to food security in rural communities, as called for in OP5. Civil society and citizen participation in ADB energy operations will promote accountability, transparency, and inclusivity, as outlined in OP6. ADB will help DMCs to secure energy for development by supporting electrification programs; promoting cleaner cooking, heating, and cooling; improving energy efficiency across supply and consumption chains; and promoting social inclusion, gender equality, and partnerships, including with civil society organizations.

Principle 2: Building a Sustainable and Resilient Energy Future

The second principle highlights the operational activities that respond to Operational Priority 3 (tackling climate change, building climate and disaster resilience, and enhancing environmental sustainability). ADB will assist DMCs in managing these critical tasks by increasing energy efficiency and the use of renewable and low-carbon energy, as well as integrating climate and disaster resilience considerations into energy sector operations. ADB will cease financing new coal-fired power and heating plants, support DMCs in achieving a planned phase-out of coal in the Asia and Pacific region, and foster a just transition that considers its impacts on people and communities. ADB's support for clean and sustainable energy solutions—such as supply and demand-side energy efficiency, renewable energy, distributed renewable energy generation, and electric mobility—will help make cities more livable by improving ambient air quality, as called for by OP3 and OP4. ADB will also support associated infrastructure such as smart and resilient power grids and battery energy storage systems to ensure the integration of an increasing share of renewable energy sources. In supporting energy infrastructure investments, ADB considers the need to maintain biodiversity and healthy ecosystems by respecting environmental safeguards.

ADB will facilitate the transition to sustainable, lower-carbon, and resilient energy systems by assisting DMCs in (i) accelerating the deployment of renewable energy, (ii) pursuing strategic decarbonization and the phase-out of coal, (iii) increasing the climate resilience of energy infrastructure and ensuring a just transition, and (iv) decoupling and/or delinking environmental degradation from energy sector projects by prioritizing ecologically friendly technologies.

Principle 3: Supporting Institutions, Private Sector Participation, and Good Governance

The third principle contributes to Operational Priority 6 by strengthening governance and institutional capacity. Universal access, climate goals, and technological innovations are accelerating change in power generation. ADB will support associated energy sector reforms such as strengthening regulatory frameworks and introducing competitive markets and market-based instruments, including carbon pricing. Strengthening DMCs' institutions will allow them to manage the sector efficiently, introduce progressive and enabling energy policies, attract private sector investment, and achieve the long-term financial sustainability of energy entities by ensuring the financial viability of investments and the maintenance of infrastructure assets. This principle also recognizes that good governance includes environmental and social considerations, supported by inclusive energy policy development. Energy generation, transmission, and distribution companies should adopt corporate policies and procedures on pollution control and waste management, health and safety, community engagement, and gender equality. Throughout this work, ADB will continue to operate consistently with the G20 Principles for Quality Infrastructure Investment, which also support OP3, emphasizing the importance of integrating economic efficiency, environmental and social considerations, climate resilience, and stricter governance in all operations.

Principle 4: Promoting Regional Cooperation and Integration

The fourth principle—fostering regional cooperation and integration—is an operational priority of Strategy 2030 (Operational Priority 7). ADB will promote regional cooperation through policy dialogue, knowledge sharing, and investments in electricity and natural gas network infrastructure and cross-border energy trading, such as building regional energy markets. The key benefit of subregional and bilateral energy cooperation is the optimal use of energy resources in the region leading to cost savings, reduced GHG emissions and air pollution, and increased energy security by enabling more diverse energy mixes and ecologically friendly T&D networks.

Principle 5: Integrated Cross-Sector Operations to Maximize Development Impact

The principle of integrated solutions responds to Strategy 2030's aim for ADB to be stronger, better, and faster in its delivery and to maximize the development impacts of cross-sector operations. ADB will integrate its energy expertise across sectors and themes to address more complex development challenges, such as water–energy–food, energy–transport, and energy–urban nexuses. It will continue to combine finance, knowledge, and partnerships in its energy operations. Its country focused approach will deliver integrated energy and cross-sector solutions that provide comprehensive and magnified development impacts.

Increasingly, clients are looking to ADB for support in areas that pose the greatest challenges such as aging infrastructure, urbanization, institutional reform, and environmental pressures. ADB's clients are becoming increasingly advanced, and transport sector support must adapt to provide the expertise, knowledge, and insight to support them.

G. Energy Sector Results Framework

ADB's Corporate Results Framework (CRF) 2019–2024 facilitates learning and performance improvement and provides the basis for reporting on ADB's operational and organizational performance, and communication with ADB stakeholders about achievement of expected results. The CRF has four levels of indicators: Level 1 reports on development progress across Asia and the Pacific; Levels 2–4 report on ADB's development effectiveness, with Level 2 covering overall performance, Level 3 operational management, and Level 4 organization effectiveness.

The results framework for the ESDG shown in Appendix 5 uses Level 2 indicators in the most part as measurement indicators.[17]

Figure 6 summarizes the energy sector guiding principles, linked CRF and SDGs, and the outcome indicators with reported results. The Energy Sector Group will continue to monitor and improve associated outcome indicators.

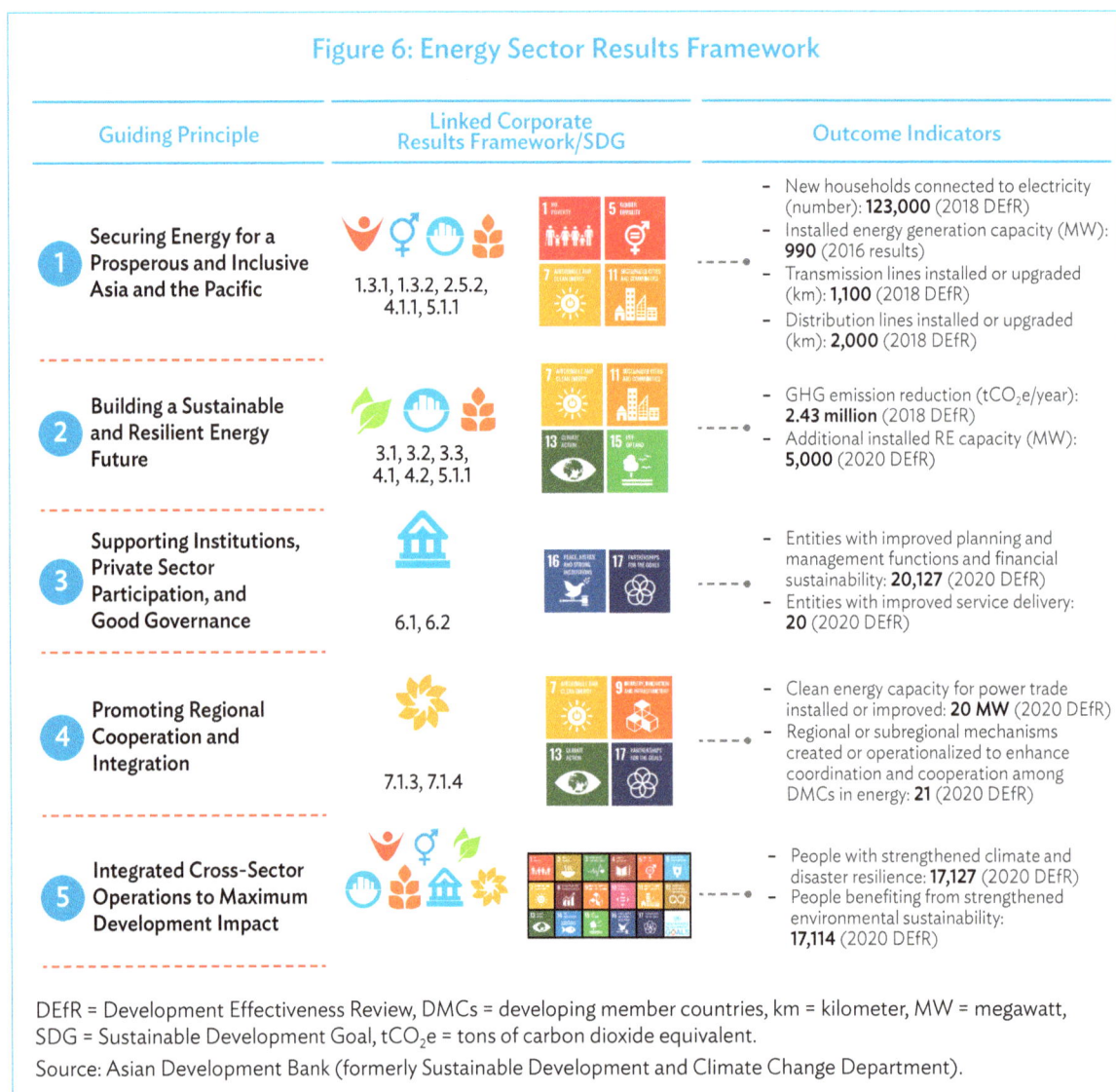

Figure 6: Energy Sector Results Framework

Guiding Principle	Linked Corporate Results Framework/SDG	Outcome Indicators
1 Securing Energy for a Prosperous and Inclusive Asia and the Pacific	1.3.1, 1.3.2, 2.5.2, 4.1.1, 5.1.1	– New households connected to electricity (number): **123,000** (2018 DEfR) – Installed energy generation capacity (MW): **990** (2016 results) – Transmission lines installed or upgraded (km): **1,100** (2018 DEfR) – Distribution lines installed or upgraded (km): **2,000** (2018 DEfR)
2 Building a Sustainable and Resilient Energy Future	3.1, 3.2, 3.3, 4.1, 4.2, 5.1.1	– GHG emission reduction (tCO$_2$e/year): **2.43 million** (2018 DEfR) – Additional installed RE capacity (MW): **5,000** (2020 DEfR)
3 Supporting Institutions, Private Sector Participation, and Good Governance	6.1, 6.2	– Entities with improved planning and management functions and financial sustainability: **20,127** (2020 DEfR) – Entities with improved service delivery: **20** (2020 DEfR)
4 Promoting Regional Cooperation and Integration	7.1.3, 7.1.4	– Clean energy capacity for power trade installed or improved: **20 MW** (2020 DEfR) – Regional or subregional mechanisms created or operationalized to enhance coordination and cooperation among DMCs in energy: **21** (2020 DEfR)
5 Integrated Cross-Sector Operations to Maximum Development Impact		– People with strengthened climate and disaster resilience: **17,127** (2020 DEfR) – People benefiting from strengthened environmental sustainability: **17,114** (2020 DEfR)

DEfR = Development Effectiveness Review, DMCs = developing member countries, km = kilometer, MW = megawatt, SDG = Sustainable Development Goal, tCO$_2$e = tons of carbon dioxide equivalent.
Source: Asian Development Bank (formerly Sustainable Development and Climate Change Department).

---

[17] A full list of CRF indicators is available at Results Framework Indicators (March 2021) and Tracking Indicators (March 2021).

WHAT WE WILL DO III

Although Asia and the Pacific has made great strides in poverty reduction and economic growth in the past decades, issues such as poverty and vulnerability, rising inequality, climate change, growing environmental pressures, and large infrastructure gaps persist. Both opportunities and challenges are being presented by technological advancement, urbanization, and changing demographics. As a trusted development partner, ADB will combine finance, knowledge, and partnerships to optimize its value addition in its support to sustainable development priorities of its DMCs.

Asia and the Pacific is responsible for more than half of the world's carbon emissions. It has also grown to rely on coal to fuel its growth as more than 80% of the increase in coal demand is projected to come from the region in the near term. This means "the battle for climate change will be won or lost in Asia and the Pacific" recognizing the place and role of the region in its bid for the clean energy transition.

The IEA has indicated that the development trajectory of emerging and developing economies in the world suggests higher emissions. Based on existing and policy announcements, emissions from this segment are projected to increase by 5 gigatons (Gt) in the next 20 years.[18] The Economist Intelligence Unit, in its latest analysis, has indicated that decarbonization will be a major challenge in the region as some countries continue to develop new coal plants despite the region being the world's largest market for renewable energy investments.[19]

This pathway can only be arrested if emissions will be decoupled from economic growth, the domestic and policy environments of these economies are improved to open the floodgate for clean energy development and the associated investments needed to support it—estimated to increase by around $1 trillion from 2021 to 2050.[20]

A. Overarching Strategic Directions

To meet DMCs' emerging needs and support the low-carbon transition, ADB is responding to the transition to an increasingly multifaceted energy sector with a forward-looking Energy Policy 2021, which will be implemented and complied with in sovereign and nonsovereign energy operations. As earlier stated, the Energy Policy 2021 is based on five policy principles, which are also the foundations of the ESDG that comprise its vision and approach (Figure 7).

---

[18] IEA. 2021. *Financing Clean Energy Transitions in Emerging and Developing Economies.* Paris.

[19] Economist Intelligence Unit. *Asia's Energy Transition—A Tough Balancing Act.* 7 September 2022.

[20] R. Gupta and J. Woetzel. 2022. *Asia's Net-Zero Transition: Opportunity and Risk Amid Climate Action.* McKinsey and Company. 29 April.

Figure 7: ADB's Energy Sector Vision and Approach

Principle 1
Securing Energy for a Prosperous and Inclusive Asia and the Pacific

Principle 2
Building a Sustainable and Resilient Energy Future

Principle 3
Supporting Institutions, Private Sector Participation, and Good Governance

Principle 4
Promoting Regional Cooperation and Integration

Principle 5
Integrated Cross-Sector Operations to Maximize Development Impact

Areas of Delivery

Decarbonization | **Decreasing energy intensity** | **Digitalization** | **Decentralization**

Note: The Energy Policy 2021 is based on five policy principles, which are also the foundations of this Energy Sector Directional Guide as depicted in the chart.

Source: Asian Development Bank (formerly Sustainable Development and Climate Change Department).

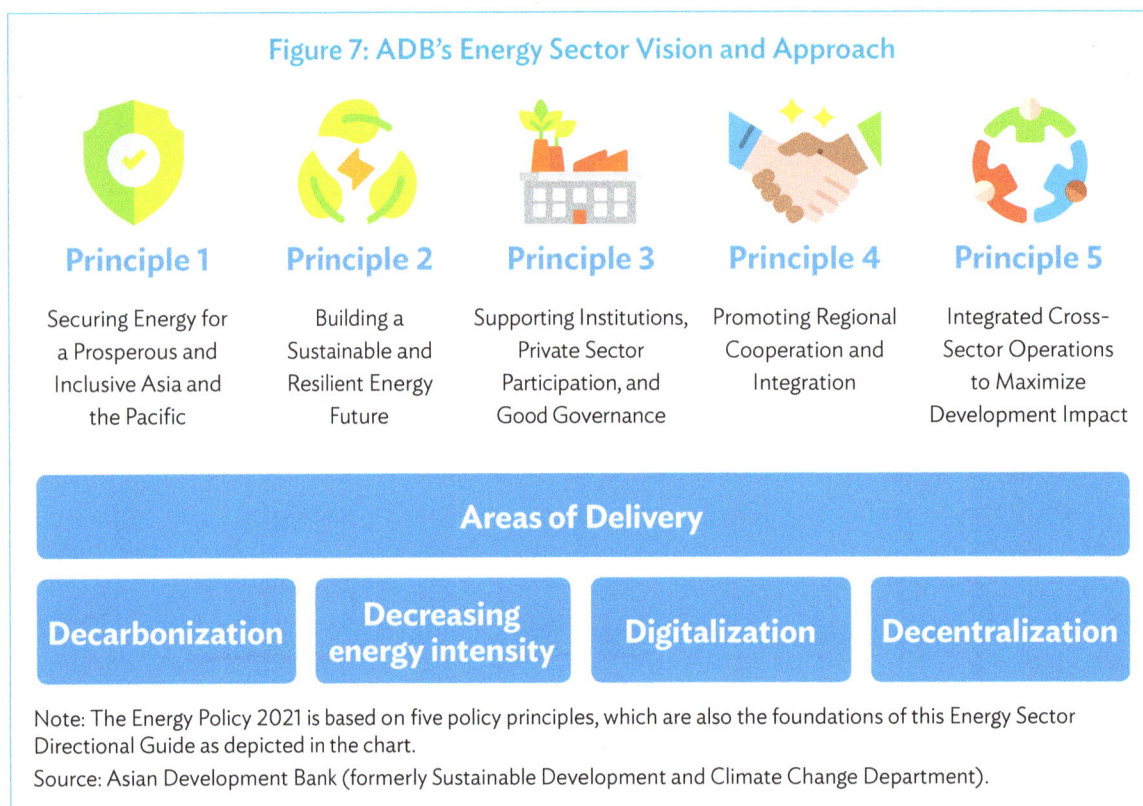

To support the energy sector vision, the implementation of the ESDG will focus on the following five areas:

1. *Confronting the Climate Change Challenge by Facilitating Just Low-Carbon Energy Transition through a Common but Differentiated Approach and Integrated Energy Planning*

A country focus in the delivery of ADB support has been a key principle of ADB's approach. The energy sector will take a common but differentiated approach to support all DMCs through finance, technical assistance, policy dialogue, and knowledge sharing to increase the ambition of their national energy plans, NDCs, and long-term climate strategies; and will encourage the low-carbon transition in the region by all means available and appropriate to national circumstances.

ADB will prioritize support for essential energy access services in the poorest and most vulnerable countries, including fragile and conflict-affected situations and small island developing states, through greater use of low-carbon and renewable energy sources, and assistance for the rehabilitation of infrastructure to enhance energy security and climate resilience. Support for a just transition will also factor in resource considerations in line with this differentiated approach. In low-income and lower-middle-income countries, ADB will continue to support reforms in the energy sector, including reforms of state-owned enterprises; the development of green and inclusive energy infrastructure to enhance productivity and competitiveness; the promotion of gender equality; and greater participation of the private sector in delivering energy infrastructure and services.

ADB will support DMCs in integrated energy planning, including revising their electrification plans, enhancing climate ambitions, phasing-out of coal in power generation, and incorporating resilience planning. ADB will assist energy planning based on a systematic analysis of technology options, costs, and social and environmental impacts. Such analysis should include three key quantitative and timebound targets: (i) decrease in CO_2 emission intensity, (ii) peaking of CO_2 emissions, and (iii) achievement of carbon neutrality. Moreover, ADB will support DMCs in integrating an assessment of climate change impacts and consequent investment considerations into their long-term energy supply strategies and national adaptation plans. ADB will seek to support appropriate policy developments that would help DMCs achieve these targets and will prioritize financing for investments identified in a long-term planning process.

2. *Supporting Developing Member Countries in Implementing Just Energy Transition and Innovative Energy Transition Mechanisms*

ADB will support developing member countries in undertaking and implementing transparent and inclusive planning and policies for a just transition. ADB will use technical assistance to assess the feasibility of early retirement of and/or repurposing coal-fired power stations, while ensuring a just transition. ADB will use blended finance to bring together market participants, philanthropy, governments, and development partners to create mechanisms that incentivize the private sector to achieve a just energy transition.

The Energy Transition Mechanism (ETM) is a promising is a promising initiative to take bold and urgent action against climate change. Market-based approaches will be leveraged by ETM to accelerate the clean energy transition through displacing fossil fuel-based power with renewable energy. Investments from the private sector, governments, multilateral banks, philanthropies, and long-term investors will finance country-specific ETM funds, (including a carbon reduction fund and a clean energy fund), for the early decommissioning of coal power assets and deployment of cleaner, renewable alternatives.[21]

As a trusted institution, ADB will support ETM and will prioritize a just transition that alleviates the potential environmental and socioeconomic impacts. ADB is initially piloting ETM in Southeast Asia in partnership with DMC governments, development partners, and the private sector, to retire or repurpose several coal-fired power plants. It is expected that ETM will be scaled up to become a carbon reduction model with real and significant impacts.

3. *Expanding Support for Demand-Side Energy Efficiency*

ADB will promote increased demand-side energy efficiency through policy support, use of innovative financing instruments, and mobilization of private sector resources. It will provide DMCs with technical assistance, grants, and loans to establish legal and regulatory frameworks, policies, and programs that support energy efficiency; and develop incentive mechanisms for consumers, utilities, energy service companies, and other market players. ADB will also assist DMCs in removing downstream and upstream barriers to energy efficiency based on their national

---

[21]   ADB. Energy Transition Mechanism.

circumstances. It will boost energy efficiency in its DMCs by collaborating with industry associations, banks, and specialized energy efficiency agencies, including providing loans for onlending under the financial intermediary loan modality. This will channel programs through locally based entities. ADB may combine financing with capacity building and technical assistance to help consolidate scattered industrial, commercial, and residential opportunities and induce behavioral changes for energy conservation.

ADB will support demand-side energy efficiency planning, in which energy efficiency targets and plans should be carefully designed to meet the needs of individual DMCs in line with their implementation capabilities. ADB will promote minimum energy performance standards for appliances and equipment, fuel economy standards for vehicles, standards for electric motors in industry, mandatory energy audits, and energy management policies for large industrial and commercial companies and building codes. They will take into consideration affordability for the targeted consumer group, given the trade-offs between the higher first costs of more efficient buildings, vehicles, and appliances versus the benefits that accrue later through better energy efficiency.

4. *Supporting Digitalization and Smart Power Systems for Increased Clean Energy Development Including Demand–Response and Efficient Power System Management*

The integration of renewable energies into existing systems calls for the reinforcement of ancillary services through energy storage, digitalization, and other innovative technologies, as well as grid management. With advanced capability of data intelligence, information processing, autonomous systems, decision-making, and power system management, digitalization and smart technologies play a key role in supporting clean energy development in renewable energy integration, decentralized energy systems, supply and demand-side energy efficiency, and demand–response.

ADB will work to accelerate the provision of energy for all as well as the low-carbon transition through the deployment and transfer of a wide range of technological innovations. It will promote the adoption of distributed systems and mini-grids to reach underserved areas. ADB will help deploy digital technologies such as smart meters to reduce technical and commercial losses and encourage demand-side energy efficiency; peer-to-peer trading using blockchain technology for energy markets; and artificial intelligence for predictive grid management and grid resilience. ADB may also support the use of advanced conductors, dynamic line rating, advanced grid control systems such as anti-blackout technology, various demand–response mechanisms, on-grid electricity storage, distributed generation, cybersecurity, and digital smart grid solutions, which are among the available options to increase grid reliability, flexibility, and resilience.

5. *Leverage Advanced Clean Energy Technologies and Commercial Financing to Accelerate the Energy Transition through One ADB Approach, Innovative Financing Mechanisms, and Business Models and Decentralized Energy Systems*

ADB's Strategy 2030 identified the One ADB approach as a tool to bring together knowledge and expertise across the organization to effectively implement and deliver its 2030 operational priorities. As the low-carbon transition will face more complex development challenges that cut through sector and thematic boundaries, ADB will integrate its energy expertise across sectors and themes to address the complex development challenges and will continue to combine finance, knowledge, and partnerships in its energy operations.

A country focus in the delivery of ADB support has been a key principle of ADB's approach. Strategy 2030 identified the country partnership strategy (CPS) as "the primary platform for defining ADB's operational focus in a country" and assigns to resident missions a central role in the implementation of corporate strategy as "the single window for country counterparts for all ADB products and services." Resident missions also have a key role to bring together regional departments and PSOD to achieve better outcomes. It is therefore imperative that the energy sector work closely with resident missions to sharpen country focus in developing and delivering CPSs, programs, and projects. The energy group will support resident missions with staffing, knowledge, training, and other resources.

ADB will invest in and raise climate finance such as green bonds and other sustainability-linked debt and equity instruments for governments and the private sector. ADB can co-invest in green bond funds and provide credit enhancement to new issuances to realize clean energy investments in the region. Its management of risk exposures, particularly through guarantees, will help involve financial institutions with a longer-term horizon—such as pension funds and insurers—in sustainable energy projects. ADB will also seek to work with impact investors that are interested in developing green portfolios in the Asia and Pacific region. With the support of development partners, ADB established the Clean Energy Financing Partnership Facility to facilitate the deployment of new, more efficient clean energy technologies, and assist policy, regulatory, and institutional reforms that encourage clean energy development. ADB will continue to partner with other development and energy institutions.

ADB will support DMCs in developing their domestic markets for clean energy financing. A long-term sustainable solution would be to develop the depth and liquidity of domestic finance sectors, with the aim of creating a balanced mix of domestic and international finance flows to pursue energy efficiency and low-carbon energy. ADB is committed to helping DMCs develop their domestic capital markets by issuing local currency bonds and through other financial products, sound structuring and pricing of both sovereign and nonsovereign projects, and through policy dialogues.

ADB will use financial intermediation as an approach to supporting dispersed subprojects. Financial intermediary loans can be used for expanding electrification, clean cooking, island energy supply, demand-side energy efficiency programs, and other programs that are not amenable to project loans or other investment modalities. ADB will apply the financial intermediary loan modality by partnering with national banks and specialized financial institutions.

ADB will champion the use of new business models and financing solutions to overcome economic constraints on complex projects. It will also promote private sector participation, including local community investments, in electrification programs. It will complement its own resources and expertise by partnering with other development partners and civil society organizations in the design and execution of energy access investment programs.

ADB will promote the adoption of distributed systems and mini-grids to reach underserved areas and support the integration of distributed renewable energy into the electricity systems. ADB will support DMCs to set standards for decentralized energy systems and interconnection requirements to reduce technical and legal barriers, as well as support capacity building to create a skilled labor force locally. ADB will support innovative financing and business models to scale up decentralized renewable energy systems in last-mile electrification. Moreover, ADB will also support sector reforms and an enabling institutional structure to transform the market to support the participation of local governments, community cooperatives, and private businesses.

ADB will operationalize the G20 Principles for Quality Infrastructure Investment in the energy sector in line with ADB's own quality infrastructure methodology development. This will help simultaneously address the unfinished development agendas of narrowing infrastructure deficits and growing environmental pressures in the sector. Technologies that enable ecologically sensitive project siting, design, construction, and operation will gain prominence, and help catalyze project approval and financing. Project components such as e-sensitivity mapping, e-flow, and life cycle assessments; and project features such as ecologically friendly linear T&D systems and fish passages in hydroelectric facilities will be supported. ADB will champion air quality management with its climate co-benefits through its programs promoting access to clean fuels and technologies; and will help enable a circular-based economy (vs. fossil-based economy) through its biomass programs.

B. ADB Additionality

With over 50 years' experience in Asia and the Pacific, ADB is a trusted development partner in the region. ADB will combine finance, knowledge, and partnerships to optimize its value addition in its support to the sustainable development priorities of its DMCs. As a leading multilateral development institution, ADB's operations strive to address market failures without distorting or crowding out the private sector markets.

ADB will prioritize support for essential energy access services in the poorest and most vulnerable countries, including fragile and conflict-affected situations and small island developing states, through greater use of low-carbon and renewable energy sources, and assistance for the rehabilitation of infrastructure to enhance energy security and climate resilience. In low-income and lower-middle-income countries, ADB will continue to support reforms in the energy sector, including reforms of state-owned enterprises; the development of green and inclusive energy infrastructure to enhance productivity and competitiveness; the promotion of gender equality; and greater participation of the private sector in delivering energy infrastructure and services.

ADB will continue to provide innovative financing and mobilize resources from private sources to support the low-carbon transition. ADB will use its unique position and financial instruments to help governments and investors mitigate risks. ADB will support DMCs to improve sector governance to accommodate innovative technologies, financing and business models, and private sector participation. ADB will promote improved policies and provide expertise in environmental, social, and governance standards, and integrity and procurement best practice.

Energy sector operations will reinforce policy dialogues, sector reforms, technical assistance, knowledge creation and sharing, gender mainstreaming, promotion of inclusiveness, capacity building, and private sector participation to maximize development impacts.

C. Implementation and Next Steps

1. Guidance Notes on Natural Gas, Large Hydropower, and Waste to Energy

ADB will be selective in its support for natural gas, large hydropower, and waste-to-energy projects. The Energy Sector Group will make available staff guidance with screening criteria for ADB operations involving natural gas, large hydropower, and waste-to-energy projects. The staff guidance notes will be updated, as needed, to reflect the criteria set forth in the joint methodology developed by the Multilateral Development Bank Working Group on Paris Alignment, in ADB's updated Energy Policy 2021, safeguard policy, and any other relevant policy.

2. Technical Assistance and Staff Resources

Implementation will require sufficient human and financial resources. Technical assistance projects will be focused and targeted at demonstrating technical and economic viability of low-carbon technologies; leveraging investments in clean energy; implementing innovative financing approaches, modalities, and instruments; and preparing these projects for ADB financing.

ADB staff skills set and technical capacity will be enhanced to meet the increasing demand for specific expertise in demand-side energy efficiency, information communication technology applications in network design and operations, and emerging low-carbon technologies (e.g., green ammonia and hydrogen, ocean energy, and energy storage).

Energy sector operations will sustain One ADB approach that it has demonstrated successfully in various projects collaborated among sovereign and nonsovereign operations, across different sectors, and between operations and knowledge departments.

3. Review of the Energy Sector Directional Guide

The ESDG is a living document and will be updated as needed. It is expected that a review will be conducted following the midterm review of the Energy Policy 2021 in 2025.

APPENDIX 1
ADB Energy Sector Knowledge Products

Table A1.1: Selected Knowledge Products in the Energy Sector, 2012–2022

Date	Product Type	Title
1-Jan-12	Publication	Sector Briefing on Climate Change Impacts and Adaptation: Energy
24-Apr-12	Case Study	Investing in Solar Energy in Asia
1-Mar-13	Publication	2012 Clean Energy Investments: Project Summaries
1-Oct-13	Publication	Energy Outlook for Asia and the Pacific (2013)
1-Nov-13	Publication	Energy Policy Options for Sustainable Development in Bangladesh
1-Dec-13	Publication	Maximizing Access to Energy for the Poor in Developing Asia
1-Dec-13	Publication	Energy Access and Energy Security in Asia and the Pacific
1-Jan-14	Publication	2013 Clean Energy Investments: Project Summaries
1-Feb-14	Publication	A Safe Space for Humanity: The Nexus of Food, Water, Energy, and Climate
1-Apr-14	Publication	Pacific and Caribbean Conference on Effective Regulation of Energy and Water Services: Conference Materials
1-Apr-14	Publication	Opportunity Cost of Natural Gas Subsidies in Bangladesh
1-May-14	Publication	Attaining Sustainable Energy Access for All: Third Asia-Pacific Dialogue on Clean Energy Governance, Policy, Law, and Regulation
1-May-14	Publication	Nepal: The National Monitoring and Evaluation System and the SREP Investment Plan
19-Jun-15	Case Study	People's Republic of China: Switching on to Clean Energy
1-Aug-14	Publication	Asia's Energy Challenge: Key Issues and Policy Options
1-Aug-14	Publication	Diversification of Energy Supply: Prospects for Emerging Energy Sources
1-Sep-14	Publication	Power Sector in Developing Asia: Current Status and Policy Issues
1-Oct-14	Publication	News from Nepal: A Quarterly Newsletter of the Nepal Resident Mission of the Asian Development Bank (October 2014)
1-Feb-15	Publication	25 Years on the Ground: ADB–Nepal Partnership for Inclusive Development
1-Mar-15	Publication	Policy Enablers for New Wind Energy Markets
1-Apr-15	Publication	Unlocking Indonesia's Geothermal Potential
1-May-15	Publication	India: Madhya Pradesh Power Sector Investment Program
1-Jun-15	Publication	2014 Clean Energy Investments: Project Summaries
1-Jun-15	Publication	Clean Energy Program: Accelerating Low-Carbon Development in Asia and the Pacific Region
1-Jun-15	Publication	Sustainable Energy Access Planning: A Framework
1-Jul-15	Publication	Business Models to Realize the Potential of Renewable Energy and Energy Efficiency in the Greater Mekong Subregion
1-Jul-15	Publication	Renewable Energy Developments and Potential in the Greater Mekong Subregion
1-Jul-15	Publication	Energy Efficiency Developments and Potential Energy Savings in the Greater Mekong Subregion

continued on next page

Table A1.1 *continued*

Date	Product Type	Title
1-Jul-15	Publication	How Strategic Environmental Assessment Can Influence Power Development Plans: Comparing Alternative Energy Scenarios for Power Planning in the Greater Mekong Subregion
1-Jul-15	Publication	Identifying Sustainability Indicators of Strategic Environmental Assessment for Power Planning
1-Aug-15	Publication	Cross-Border Power Trading in South Asia: A Techno Economic Rationale
1-Sep-15	Publication	Sustainable Energy for All Status Report: Tracking Progress in Asia and the Pacific—A Summary Report
1-Sep-15	Publication	Improving Energy Efficiency and Reducing Emissions through Intelligent Railway Station Buildings
1-Oct-15	Publication	Fossil Fuel Subsidies in Thailand: Trends, Impacts, and Reforms
1-Oct-15	Publication	Fossil Fuel Subsidies in Indonesia: Trends, Impacts, and Reforms
1-Oct-15	Publication	Knowledge and Power: Lessons from ADB Energy Projects
1-Dec-15	Publication	Investing In Renewable Energy Generation and Power Transmission in Eastern Indonesia
1-Dec-15	Publication	Making Renewable Energy a Success in Bangladesh: Getting the Business Model Right
1-Jan-16	Publication	Southeast Asia and the Economics of Global Climate Stabilization
26-Jan-16	Case Study	Using Water as Fuel: Pakistan's Ranolia Hydropower Project
1-Mar-16	Publication	Fossil Fuel Subsidies in Asia: Trends, Impacts, and Reforms – Integrative Report
1-Mar-16	Publication	Achieving Universal Electricity Access in Indonesia
28-Mar-16	Case Study	PRC's Tianjin Breathing Easier with Cleaner Coal Power
1-Apr-16	Publication	Outlook for Increased Adoption of Smart Grid Technologies in ADB Energy Sector Operations
1-Apr-16	Publication	Emissions Trading Schemes and Their Linking: Challenges and Opportunities in Asia and the Pacific
1-May-16	Publication	2015 Clean Energy Investments: Project Summaries
1-Jun-16	Publication	Going Beyond the Meter: Inclusive Energy Solutions in South Asia—Conference Report
7-Jun-16	Case Study	Sun, Partnerships Power Thailand Solar Project
20-Jun-16	Case Study	In the People's Republic of China, Manure is Being Turned into Money
1-Jul-16	Publication	Cleantech Start-ups Can Solve Climate Change
1-Aug-16	Publication	Improving Regulatory Environment for a Regional Power Market in South Asia
1-Sep-16	Publication	Bangladesh: Consolidating Export-led Growth—Country Diagnostic Study
1-Oct-16	Publication	Improving Energy Efficiency in South Asia
20-Oct-16	Case Study	State-of-the-art Technology Boosts Energy Efficiency, Saves Money at One of Uzbekistan's Largest Plants
17-Nov-16	Case Study	Lao PDR Weaves a Renewable Energy Future
1-Dec-16	Publication	Samoa: Alaoa Hydropower Refurbishment—Pacific Project Brief
1-Dec-16	Publication	Samoa: Fiaga Diesel Power Plant—Pacific Project Brief
1-Dec-16	Publication	Samoa: Transmission and Distribution Upgrade—Pacific Project Brief
1-Dec-16	Publication	Samoa: Prepayment Meter Rollout—Pacific Project Brief

continued on next page

Table A1.1 *continued*

Date	Product Type	Title
1-Dec-16	Publication	Vanuatu: Luganville Grid-connected Solar Power Trial—Pacific Project Brief
1-Dec-16	Publication	Solomon Islands: Auki Coconut Oil Biofuel Trial—Pacific Project Brief
1-Jan-17	Publication	District Cooling in the People's Republic of China: Status and Development Potential
1-Jan-17	Publication	Green Growth Opportunities for Asia
1-Feb-17	Publication	Impact of Fukushima Nuclear Disaster on Oil-Consuming Sectors of Japan
1-Feb-17	Publication	Energy Storage in Grids with High Penetration of Variable Generation
1-Feb-17	Publication	Bangladesh: Development Effectiveness Brief
1-Mar-17	Publication	Earth Observation for a Transforming Asia and Pacific
1-Apr-17	Publication	Emerging Indonesian Data Center Market and Energy Efficiency Opportunities
27-Apr-17	Case Study	Expanding Access to Affordable Electricity in Cambodia
1-May-17	Publication	LED Street Lighting Best Practices
1-Jul-17	Publication	Quantifying Water and Energy Linkages in Irrigation: Experiences from Viet Nam
1-Jul-17	Publication	Alternatives to Bank Finance: Role of Carbon Tax and Hometown Investment Trust Funds in Developing Green Energy Projects in Asia
1-Aug-17	Publication	The Internet of Things in the Power Sector: Opportunities in Asia and the Pacific
1-Aug-17	Publication	Geographic Information System-Based Decision Support System for Renewable Energy Development: An Indonesian Case Study
1-Sep-17	Publication	Papua New Guinea: Kimbe-Biala Transmission Line—Pacific Project Brief
1-Sep-17	Publication	Fiji: Tropical Cyclone Winston Emergency Reconstruction Response—Pacific Project Brief
1-Oct-17	Publication	Harmonizing Electricity Laws in South Asia
1-Oct-17	Publication	Reaching Scale in Access to Energy: Lessons from Practitioners
1-Dec-17	Publication	Water–Energy Nexus in the People's Republic of China and Emerging Issues
1-Dec-17	Publication	Pathways to Low-Carbon Development for the Philippines
1-Dec-17	Publication	Pathways to Low-Carbon Development for Viet Nam
1-Dec-17	Publication	Future Carbon Fund Delivering Co-Benefits for Sustainable Development
15-Jan-18	Case Study	Indonesia: Muara Laboh Geothermal Power
15-Jan-18	Case Study	Azerbaijan: Shah Deniz Gas Field Expansion
1-Feb-18	Publication	Gender Equality Results Case Study: India—Enhancing Energy-Based Livelihoods for Women Micro-Entrepreneurs
22-Feb-18	Case Study	Darkness Gone with the Wind in Nepal
1-May-18	Publication	Green Energy Finance in Australia and New Zealand
1-Jun-18	Case Study	New Generators Provide Reliable, Affordable Electricity in Nauru
1-Jul-18	Publication	The Impact of Nationally Determined Contributions on the Energy Sector: Implications for ADB and Its Developing Member Countries
1-Aug-18	Publication	Green Energy Finance in India: Challenges and Solutions
1-Aug-18	Publication	Implications of Fiscal and Financial Policies for Unlocking Green Finance and Green Investment
1-Aug-18	Publication	Sustainable Energy Access Planning: A Case Study
1-Sep-18	Publication	Energy Market Liberalization for Unlocking Community-Based Green Finance

continued on next page

Table A1.1 *continued*

Date	Product Type	Title
1-Sep-18	Publication	A "Cap and Invest" Strategy for Managing the Intergenerational Burden of Financing Energy Transitions
1-Sep-18	Publication	Infrastructure Financing in South Asia
1-Sep-18	Publication	Asian Development Review: Volume 35, Number 2
1-Oct-18	Publication	Energy Efficiency Finance Programs: Best Practices to Leverage Private Green Finance
1-Oct-18	Publication	Green Finance in Pakistan: Barriers and Solutions
1-Oct-18	Publication	Energy Technology Innovation in South Asia: Implications for Gender Equality and Social Inclusion
1-Oct-18	Publication	Tariff Appraisal Study: Balancing Sustainability and Efficiency with Inclusive Access
1-Nov-18	Publication	Impacts of Fiscal Policy on Green Technologies Transfer
1-Nov-18	Publication	Social Funding of Green Financing: An Application of Distributed Ledger Technologies
1-Nov-18	Publication	50 Climate Solutions from Cities in the People's Republic of China
1-Nov-18	Publication	Together We Deliver: Results Achieved, Lives Improved
8-Nov-18	Case Study	India: Harvesting the Results of a Reliable Power Supply in Madhya Pradesh
8-Nov-18	Case Study	Samoa: Rebounding Together from Dual Crises
1-Dec-18	Publication	Handbook on Battery Energy Storage System
1-Dec-18	Publication	Creating an Enabling Environment for Public–Private Partnerships in Waste-to-Energy Projects
1-Dec-18	Publication	Smart Metering Road Map for Nepal
1-Dec-18	Publication	A Model for Utilizing Spillover Taxes and Community-Based Funds to Fill the Green Energy Financing Gap in Asia
1-Dec-18	Publication	Greater Mekong Subregion: Twenty-Five Years of Partnership
1-Jan-19	Publication	Realizing the Potential of Public–Private Partnerships to Advance Asia's Infrastructure Development
1-Apr-19	Publication	Impact Evaluation of Energy Interventions: A Review of the Evidence
3-Apr-19	Case Study	Investing in Asia's Maiden Green Bonds
1-May-19	Case Study	The Pacific Islands: The Push for Renewable Energy
1-Jun-19	Publication	International Conference on Energy 4.0: Designing the Future of Thailand's Power Sector—Event Summary
1-Jul-19	Publication	Solar District Heating in the People's Republic of China: Status and Development Potential
1-Aug-19	Publication	Guidebook for Deploying Distributed Renewable Energy Systems: A Case Study on the Cobrador Hybrid Solar PV Mini-Grid
1-Aug-19	Publication	Renewable Energy in Central Asian Economies: Role in Reducing Regional Energy Insecurity
1-Aug-19	Publication	Energy Insecurity and Renewable Energy Sources: Prospects and Challenges for Azerbaijan
1-Sep-19	Publication	Managing Nepal's Dudh Koshi River System for a Fair and Sustainable Future
1-Sep-19	Publication	Kyrgyz Republic: Improving Growth Potential
1-Oct-19	Publication	Electric Vehicles and Energy Insecurity in ASEAN Countries: Renewable Energy Integration and Urban Air Quality

continued on next page

Table A1.1 *continued*

Date	Product Type	Title
1-Oct-19	Publication	Achieving Energy Security in Asia: Diversification, Integration and Policy Implications
1-Oct-19	Publication	Azerbaijan and ADB (1999–2019): 20 Years of Partnership
1-Nov-19	Publication	Avoiding Energy Insecurity by Promoting Private Investment—The Case of the Vietnamese Power Sector
1-Nov-19	Publication	State Ownership and Nationalization in Energy Sector: The Case of Kazakhstan's Oil Industry
1-Nov-19	Publication	Renewable Energy Financing Schemes for Indonesia
1-Dec-19	Publication	Energy Insecurity in Turkey: Opportunities for Renewable Energy
1-Dec-19	Publication	Dimensions of Energy Insecurity on Small Islands: The Case of the Maldives
1-Dec-19	Publication	Does Regulation Promote Sustainable Development Outcomes? Empirical Evidence from the Indian Electricity Sector
1-Feb-20	Publication	Harmonizing Power Systems in the Greater Mekong Subregion: Regulatory and Pricing Measures to Facilitate Trade
1-Feb-20	Publication	Unlocking Innovation for Development
1-Feb-20	Publication	Analyzing the Falling Solar and Wind Tariffs: Evidence from India
1-Mar-20	Publication	Analyzing the Factors Influencing the Demand and Supply of Solar Modules in Japan
1-Mar-20	Publication	Energy Insecurity and Renewable Energy Policy: Comparison between the People's Republic of China and Japan
1-Mar-20	Publication	The Energy–Pollution–Health Nexus: A Panel Data Analysis of Low- and Middle-Income Asian Nations
1-Mar-20	Publication	Asian Development Review: Volume 37, Number 1
1-Jun-20	Publication	Asia and the Pacific Renewable Energy Status Report
1-Jun-20	Publication	Mongolia's Economic Prospects: Resource-Rich and Landlocked between Two Giants
13-Jul-20	Case Study	A Power of Good: How ADB's Climate-Resilient Investment Is Boosting Tonga's Energy Future
1-Aug-20	Publication	The Role of Fiscal Incentives in Promoting Energy Efficiency in the Industrial Sector: Case Studies from Asia
1-Aug-20	Publication	A Study on the Prospect of Hydropower to Hydrogen in Nepal
1-Aug-20	Publication	What Are the Determinants of Fuel Subsidies in Asia-Pacific Economic Cooperation Countries?
1-Aug-20	Publication	Unleashing Market-Based Approaches to Drive Energy Efficiency Interventions in India: An Analysis of the Perform, Achieve, Trade (PAT) Scheme
1-Sep-20	Publication	Renewable Energy Tariffs and Incentives in Indonesia: Review and Recommendations
1-Sep-20	Publication	Off-Balance-Sheet Equity: The Engine for Energy Efficiency Capital Mobilization
1-Sep-20	Publication	The Viability of Green Bonds as a Financing Mechanism for Green Buildings in ASEAN
1-Sep-20	Publication	Energy Prices and the Economic Feasibility of Using Hydrogen Energy for Road Transport in the People's Republic of China
1-Sep-20	Publication	Electricity Cross-Subsidies in the People's Republic of China: Equity, Reverse Ramsey Pricing, and Welfare Analysis
1-Oct-20	Publication	Energy Infrastructure for Decarbonizing Other Energy Sectors through Renewable Electricity – A Spatio-Temporal Analysis from Useful Energy Demand to Renewable Energy Supply of Sector Coupling Pathways Based on the German Case

continued on next page

Table A1.1 *continued*

Date	Product Type	Title
1-Oct-20	Publication	Energy Insecurity in Asia: Challenges, Solutions, and Renewable Energy
1-Oct-20	Publication	Financing of Energy Efficiency in Public Goods: The Case of Street Lighting Systems in Indonesia
1-Oct-20	Publication	Bhutan and the Asian Development Bank – Partnership for Inclusive Growth: Development Effectiveness Brief
1-Oct-20	Publication	Green Finance Strategies for Post-COVID-19 Economic Recovery in Southeast Asia: Greening Recoveries for Planet and People
1-Nov-20	Publication	A Brighter Future for Maldives Powered by Renewables: Road Map for the Energy Sector 2020–2030
1-Nov-20	Publication	Rebalancing Subsidies in Market-Based Energy Sectors: Synergies and Obstacles in Developing and Transition Economies
1-Nov-20	Publication	Strategy for Northeast Asia Power System Interconnection
1-Nov-20	Publication	Green Finance in Bangladesh: Policies, Institutions, and Challenges
1-Dec-20	Publication	How Better Regulation Can Shape the Future of Indonesia's Electricity Sector
1-Dec-20	Publication	Transforming Power Development Planning in the Greater Mekong Subregion: A Strategic and Integrated Approach
1-Dec-20	Publication	A Review of the Strategy for the Northeast Asia Power System Interconnection
1-Dec-20	Publication	A Way Forward for Energy Pricing and Market Reforms to Reduce Emissions: The Case of the Top 10 Carbon Dioxide–Emitting Countries
1-Dec-20	Publication	Pakistan: Reviving Growth through Competitiveness
1-Jan-21	Publication	How Different Electricity Pricing Systems Affect the Energy Trilemma: Assessing Indonesia's Electricity Market Transition
1-Jan-21	Publication	Increasing Access to Clean Cooking in the Philippines: Challenges and Prospects
1-Jan-21	Publication	Cross-Economy Dynamics in Energy Productivity: Evidence from 47 Economies over the Period 2000–2015
1-Jan-21	Publication	How Precious Is the Reliability of the Residential Electricity Service in Developing Economies? Evidence from India
1-Jan-21	Publication	Analysis of Forecasting Models in an Electricity Market under Volatility
1-Feb-21	Publication	Carbon Capture, Utilization, and Storage Game Changers in Asia: 2020 Compendium of Technologies and Enablers
1-Feb-21	Publication	COVID-19 Impact on Micro, Small, and Medium-Sized Enterprises under the Lockdown: Evidence from a Rapid Survey in the Philippines
1-Mar-21	Publication	Office of the Special Project Facilitator's Lessons Learned: Sri Lanka Clean Energy and Network Efficiency Investment Project
1-Mar-21	Publication	The Role of Captive Power Plants in the Bangladesh Electricity Sector
23-Mar-21	Case Study	Solar Power from the Rooftops in Sri Lanka
1-Apr-21	Publication	Screening Tool for Energy Evaluation of Projects: A Reference Guide for Assessing Water Supply and Wastewater Treatment Systems
1-Apr-21	Publication	Rooftop Solar Development in India: Measuring Policies and Mapping Business Models
1-May-21	Publication	Infrastructure and Firm Performance in CAREC Countries: Cross-Sectional Evidence at the Firm Level
26-May-21	Case Study	Helping Sri Lanka to Go Green

continued on next page

Table A1.1 *continued*

Date	Product Type	Title
1-Jun-21	Publication	100 Climate Actions from Cities in Asia and the Pacific
1-Jul-21	Publication	COVID-19 and Energy Sector Development in Asia and the Pacific: Guidance Note
1-Jul-21	Publication	Financing Clean Energy in Developing Asia
1-Jul-21	Publication	The Value of Unmanned Aerial Systems for Power Utilities in Developing Asia
1-Jul-21	Publication	Oil Price Shocks and Green Bonds: A Longitudinal Multilevel Model
18-Oct-21	Case Study	Power to the Poor Scheme Empowers Rural Women in the Lao PDR
1-Nov-21	Publication	Just Transition Beyond the Energy Sector
1-Nov-21	Publication	Lessons Learned from Compliance Reviews at the Asian Development Bank (2004–2020): Mundra Ultra Mega Power Project in India
1-Nov-21	Publication	Improving Skills for the Electricity Sector in Indonesia
1-Dec-21	Publication	Pacific Energy Update 2021
1-Dec-21	Publication	Energy Efficiency in South Asia: Opportunities for Energy Sector Transformation
1-Feb-22	Publication	Inclusive Community Energy Resilience in Bangladesh
1-Mar-22	Publication	Mitigating Energy Shortages in the People's Republic of China
1-Mar-22	Publication	Clean Heating Technologies: A Pilot Project Case Study from Northern People's Republic of China
1-May-22	Publication	Making Urban Power Distribution Systems Climate-Resilient
1-May-22	Publication	Lessons Learned from Compliance Reviews at the Asian Development Bank (2004–2020): Visayas Base-Load Power Development Project in the Philippines
1-Jun-22	Publication	Exploiting Complementarity of Carbon Pricing Instruments for Low-Carbon Development in the People's Republic of China
1-Jun-22	Publication	The Cold Economy
1-Jul-2022	Publication	Promoting Green Buildings: Barriers, Solutions, and Policies
1-Jul-2022	Publication	The Story of Lanka Electricity Company
1-Aug-22	Publication	Road Map Update for Carbon Capture, Utilization, and Storage Demonstration and Deployment in the People's Republic of China
1-Aug-22	Publication	Hybrid and Battery Energy Storage Systems: Review and Recommendations for Pacific Island Projects

Note: ADB Energy Sector knowledge work also encompasses articles, blog posts, infographics, opinion editorials, and videos.
Source: Asian Development Bank (formerly Sustainable Development and Climate Change Department).

APPENDIX 2
ADB Energy Sector Training and Capacity Development Program

Table A2.1: Flagship Events

Year	Date	Title
2013	25–28 June	Asia Clean Energy Forum 2013: Unlocking Asia's Clean Energy Future
2014	16–20 June	Asia Clean Energy Forum 2014: Connecting the Policy, Technology and Finance Communities
2015	15–19 June	Asia Clean Energy Forum 2015: Connecting the Policy, Technology and Finance Communities
2016	6 –10 June	Asia Clean Energy Forum 2016: Gearing up for the Post-COP21 Era of Implementation Showcasing Clean Energy Innovations
2017	5–8 June	Asia Clean Energy Forum 2017: The Future is Here – Achieving Universal Access and Climate Targets
2018	4– 8 June	Asia Clean Energy Forum 2018: Harnessing Innovation to Power the Future
2019	17–21 June	Asia Clean Energy Forum 2019: Partnering for Impact
2020	15–19 June	Asia Clean Energy Forum 2020: Vision 20/20 – Cross-sectoral Innovations for a Sustainable Future
2021	14–18 June	Asia Clean Energy Forum 2021: Accelerating the Low-Carbon Transition in Asia and the Pacific
2022	14–17 June	Asia Clean Energy Forum 2022: Innovative and Integrated Solutions for a Low-Carbon and Resilient Future

Source: Asian Development Bank (formerly Sustainable Development and Climate Change Department).

Table A2.2: Selected Knowledge Sharing Events and Brownbags

Year	Date	Title
2017	22 February	Energy Storage: State of Charge by General Electric
2017	8 March	The Policy and Technical Design for Renewable Energy Integration – an Électricité de France presentation
2017	24 March	Smart Metering and Grid Sensoring Platform by Network Energy Services
2017	24 March	Green Solutions for Lighting and Energy – an EBRD presentation
2017	29 March	The Role of Asia in the Future of Global Energy – by Fatih Birol, IEA
2017	2 May	Demand-Side Smart Grid Applications by Susumu Yoneoka
2017	20 June	Hydrogen Production for Electricity Generation and Off-grid Application by Toshiba Japan
2017	22 June	Cutting Transmission Losses Using Aluminum Conductor Fiber Reinforced (ACFR) Lines by Mitsui & Co., Ltd
2017	27 June	Energy Storage System by Dae Kyeong Kim
2017	20 July	World Energy Investment 2017 – an IEA presentation
2017	17 August	Energy Storage for Micro-grid Application – a Tesla presentation
2017	29 August	Future Mobility and Grid System by NTU Energy Research Institute
2017	17 October	Gigatech Solutions for Gigaton Programs: Sustainable Pre-Stressed Concrete from Seawater by D. Millison and S. Countryman
2017	27 October	Integrating Energy Efficiency and Renewable Energy in Buildings – a CSIRO presentation
2017	27 October	ASEAN Energy Outlook 2017 – an IEA presentation
2018	15 January	Battery Technologies and their Applications
2018	5 February	Materials Matter for Ensuring Sustainable PV Module Performance and Sustainable Project Returns by DuPont India
2018	12 February	Bio-coal Production through Torrefaction by Orange Green (Netherlands)
2018	20 February	Hydrogen Gas Technology and Its Applications by Joi Scientific (USA)
2018	13 March	Lessons from the French Utility and Transmission Operators by Électricité de France (EDF) and Philippe Michal, Réseau de Transport d'Électricité (RTE)
2018	17 April	Power Grid Monitoring System to Enhance Grid Performance by Bivee
2018	22 May	Wind and Solar Microgrids and Desalination Systems for Southeastern Asian Off-grid Markets by WindKinetic
2018	15 June	Blockchain in the Energy Sector by Reiner Lemoine Institut gGmbH
2018	30 August	Cluster-Based Electricity Supply System – a Waseda University presentation
2018	7 December	Electric Networks of Armenia's Best Practice in Efficiency and Reliable Distribution Network
2019	8 March	Gas Energy Technology – the Best Mix with Renewables by Toru Ito
2019	13 March	Making Electricity Always Available by HDF Energy
2019	19 March	Battery Energy Storage – Accelerating the World's Transition to Sustainable Energy – a Tesla presentation

continued on next page

Table A2.2 *continued*

Year	Date	Title
2019	26 March	Smart Solutions for Solar PV Technology by Huawei Solar
2019	27 March	Regional Cooperation and Renewable Energy Integration to the Grid by RTEi
2019	2 April	Geoflow Imaging for Cost-Effective Geothermal Exploration by Geoflow Imaging Ltd.
2019	23 April	Franco–Chinese Collaboration on Air-Climate-Energy Integration in the People's Republic of China
2019	22 May	Energy Optimal Planning Tool for Multi-Energy Systems Integration and Resilience by NTU
2019	27 May	Highly Optimized Low-Cost Small-Scale Wind Turbine by FlowGen
2019	20 August	Comparing Dispatchable Renewable Electricity Options by ITP Thermal (Australia)
2019	26 September	Asia-Pacific Economic Cooperation (APEC) Region Energy Demand and Supply Outlook – an APERC presentation
2019	24 October	Sustainable Deployment of Electric Vehicles in Developing Countries by TalinoEV
2020	12 February	Risks and their Mitigation in Solar Projects by Zuva Energy
2020	6 July	Optimizing Power Systems through the PLEXOS Software by the Energy Exemplar (Australia)
2020	14 July	Biodigester Technology for Clean Cooking and Sustainable Farming by ATEC Biodigester
2020	22 July	Technologies in Smart Energy and Smart Cities by Honeywell
2020	13 August	Integrated Smart Solutions for Improved Energy Services and Energy Efficiency by SN Electric Power Planning and Design Research Institute (People's Republic of China [PRC])
2020	27 August	IRENA Toolbox for Renewable Energy Grid Integration
2020	8 October	Concentrated Solar Power (CSP) Generation Solutions for the Dashoguz Area in Turkmenistan
From 2021	Various	Marine Aquaculture Reefs, Renewable Energy, and Ecotourism for Ecosystem Dataroom
2021	25 March	Mongolia First Utility-Scale Energy Storage Project
2021	8 April	Uzbekistan Power Sector Reform Program
2021	21 April	Tajikistan Power Sector Development Program
2021	7 May	PRC Air Quality Improvement in the Greater Beijing-Tianjin-Hebei Region—Green Financing Scale Up Project
2021	28 May	Uzbekistan Navoi Solar Power Project
2021	22 July	Kiribati South Tarawa Renewable Energy Project
2021	5 August	India Bengaluru Smart Energy-Efficient Power Distribution Project
2021	26 August	Palau Disaster Resilient Clean Energy Financing
2021	10 November	Thailand Southern Thailand Wind Power and Battery Energy Storage Project

Source: Asian Development Bank (formerly Sustainable Development and Climate Change Department).

Table A2.3: Training

Year	Date	Title
2013	13–15 November	Introduction to Power Systems
2013	25 –29November	Sustainable Energy Training: Energy Generation and Supply
2013	11–12 December	Energy Efficiency Policies for the Southeast Asia Region
2014	15–16 May	Energy Efficiency Regional Training-Workshop
2014	28–30 May	Energy Efficiency Policy in Central Asia
2014	5–6 June	GTMax Power System Optimization Software Training
2014	16–20 June	9th Asia Clean Energy Forum
2014	8–9 September	Regional Energy Trade Workshop
2015	4–7 March	Asia Leadership Program on Sustainable Development and Climate Change
2015	15–19 June	10th Asia Clean Energy Forum
2015	27–31 July	Asian Regional Workshop on Roadmaps for Energy Efficiency
2015	18–19 November	Clean Energy Forum of East Asia Summit: Co-Building a Greener Energy Network for Sustainable Economic Progress
2016	6–10 June	11th Asia Clean Energy Forum
2016	8–10 December	Economic Analysis of Energy Projects
2017	5–8 June	12th Asia Clean Energy Forum
2017	12–13 October	Asia-Pacific Forum on Low-Carbon Technology
2017	5–7 December	Economic Analysis of Energy Projects
2018	6–9 March	ADB and ADBI Seminar on 21st Century Energy Systems 2018
2018	4–8 June	13th Asia Clean Energy Forum: Clean Energy Day
2018	30 August–1 September	Training Program on Solar Photovoltaic Pumping Technology for Irrigation and Clean Water Supply
2018	24–26 October	Asia-Pacific Forum on Low-Carbon Technology
2018	3–5 December	Economic Analysis of Energy Projects
2019	27 February–1 March	Regional Workshop on High-Level Innovative Technologies
2019	17–21 June	14th Asia Clean Energy Forum
2019	16–18 October	Asia-Pacific Forum on Low-Carbon Technologies 2019
2019	20 November	Estimating Greenhouse Gas Emission Reduction from Energy Projects
2019	4–6 December	Economic Analysis of Energy Projects
2020	15 to 19 June	15th Asia Clean Energy Forum
2020	9–10 November	Estimating Greenhouse Gas Emission Reduction from Energy Projects
2020	2–3 December	Economic Analysis of Energy Projects
2021	7–8 December	Estimating Greenhouse Gas Emission Reduction from Energy Projects
2022	August/September	Training Sessions on Solar Photovoltaic (PV) Supply Chain Guidance Note
2022	December	Estimating Greenhouse Gas Emission Reduction from Energy Projects

Source: Asian Development Bank (formerly Sustainable Development and Climate Change Department).

ADB Energy Sector Assessments

Table A3.1: Energy Sector Assessment Documents by Developing Member Country

Month/Year	Country	Title
Apr 2013	REG	Assessment of the Greater Mekong Subregion Energy Sector Development: Progress, Prospects, and Regional Investment Priorities
Jun 2013	LAO	Lao People's Democratic Republic: Energy Sector Assessment, Strategy, and Road Map 2013 Update
Jul 2015	REG	Assessment of Power Sector Reforms in Asia: Experience of Georgia, Sri Lanka, and Viet Nam—Synthesis Report
Jul 2015	GEO	Assessment of Power Sector Reforms in Georgia: Country Report
Sep 2015	VIE	Assessment of Power Sector Reforms in Viet Nam: Country Report
Sep 2015	SRI	Assessment of Power Sector Reforms in Sri Lanka: Country Report
Dec 2015	VIE	Viet Nam: Energy Sector Assessment, Strategy, and Road Map
Jun 2016	REG	Greater Mekong Subregion Energy Sector Assessment, Strategy, and Road Map
Jul 2016	INO	Indonesia: Energy Sector Assessment, Strategy, and Road Map
Aug 2017	NEP	Nepal Energy Sector Assessment, Strategy, and Road Map
Oct 2018	PHI	Philippines: Energy Sector Assessment, Strategy, and Road Map
Dec 2018	CAM	Cambodia: Energy Sector Assessment, Strategy, and Road Map
Nov 2019	LAO	Lao People's Democratic Republic: Energy Sector Assessment, Strategy, and Road Map
Dec 2019	SRI	Sri Lanka: Energy Sector Assessment, Strategy, and Road Map
Dec 2020	INO	Indonesia Energy Sector Assessment, Strategy, and Road Map – Update

ADB = Asian Development Bank, CAM = Cambodia, GEO = Georgia, INO = Indonesia, LAO = Lao People's Democratic Republic, NEP = Nepal, PHI = Philippines, REG = Regional, SRI = Sri Lanka, VIE = Viet Nam.

Source: Asian Development Bank (formerly Sustainable Development and Climate Change Department).

APPENDIX 4
Summary of Key Energy Guidance Documents of Multilateral Development Banks

Table A4.1: Policy and Strategic Documents in Energy by Multilateral Development Bank

Energy Policy Key Documents	Policy/ Strategy/ Other	Year of Launch	Highlights and Position on Fossil Fuels
African Development Bank Energy Policy 2012 New Energy Deal for Africa 2016	Policy Strategy	2012 2016	New deal based on five principles: • Raising aspirations to solve Africa's energy challenges • Establishing the Transformative Partnership on Energy for Africa • Mobilizing domestic and international capital for innovative financing in Africa's energy sector • Supporting African governments in strengthening energy policy, regulation, and sector governance • Increasing the African Development Bank's investments in energy and climate financing. 　◦ 2012 policy does not exclude coal, oil, and gas-fired power. 　◦ Oil and gas exploration activities will not be supported.
Asian Development Bank Energy Policy 2009	Policy	2009	Three pillars: • Developing clean energy (energy efficiency, renewable energy, fuel switching) • Increasing energy access • Improving sector governance (necessary to bring in commercial investment). 　◦ Coal-fired power in exceptional cases only. 　◦ Coal mine and oil field development in exceptional cases only. 　◦ Any oil and gas field exploration will not be financed.
Asian Infrastructure Investment Bank Energy Sector Strategy: Sustainable Energy for Asia	Strategy	2018	Guiding principles: • Promote energy access and security • Realize energy efficiency potential • Reduce the carbon intensity of energy supply • Local and regional pollution management • Catalyze private capital • Promote regional cooperation and connectivity. 　◦ Oil and coal-fired power plants would be considered if they replace existing less-efficient capacity or are essential to the reliability and integrity of the system, or if no viable or affordable alternative exists in specific cases. 　◦ Oil and natural gas processing, transportation, and distribution will be supported if they improve energy security or promote regional integration and trade.
Islamic Development Bank Energy Sector Policy	Policy	2018	Four policy pillars: • Increase access to modern energy services • Scale up renewable energy • Increase energy efficiency • Improve knowledge services

continued on next page

Table A4.1 *continued*

Energy Policy Key Documents	Policy/ Strategy/ Other	Year of Launch	Highlights and Position on Fossil Fuels
European Investment Bank Energy Lending Policy	Policy	2019	Four themes: • Unlocking energy efficiency • Decarbonizing energy supply • Supporting innovative technologies and new types of energy infrastructure • Securing the enabling infrastructure 　° EIB will not support (i) the production of oil and natural gas; (ii) traditional gas infrastructure (networks, storage, refining facilities); (iii) power generation technologies resulting in greenhouse gas emissions above 250 grams of carbon dioxide per kilowatt-hour of electricity generated, averaged over the lifetime for gas-fired power plants seeking to integrate low-carbon fuels; and (iv) large-scale heat production infrastructure based on unabated oil, natural gas, coal, or peat.
European Bank for Reconstruction and Development Energy Sector Strategy 2019–2023	Strategy	2018	Four interrelated strategic directions: • Decarbonization and electrification • Well-functioning energy markets • Cleaner oil and gas value chains • Energy-efficient and inclusive economies
Memorandum Green Economy Transition Approach 2021–2025 (July 2020)	Other	2020	° No thermal coal mining or coal-fired electricity generation capacity 　° No upstream oil exploration (…) (i) increase low-carbon energy supply from renewable energy and low-carbon fuels such as hydrogen; (ii) natural gas as a transition fuel; (…) Financing activities will focus on innovative renewable energy systems and low-carbon fuel transportation and storage, utility-scale storage and the upgrade of gas and hydrogen transportation infrastructure.
Inter-American Development Bank (IADB)			Thematic lines: • Energy access–coverage, quality, reliability, and affordability in the provision of energy services. • Energy sustainability–energy efficiency, renewable energy, and climate change mitigation and adaptation, and reduction of environmental impacts in the long term. • Energy security–energy infrastructure and regional energy integration for the provision of reliable services. • Energy governance–institutions, regulation, policies, and information to foster the sector's long-term economic and financial sustainability.
Energy Sector Framework Document	Other	2018	IADB will give a lower priority to fossil fuel technologies, unless the investments make sense from an economic standpoint taking externalities into account, for example: in the rehabilitation of existing plants, substitution of solid or liquid fossil with cleaner gaseous fossil fuels; or to meet the demand for energy services.
Environmental and Social Policy Framework	Other	2020	IADB will not finance Activities that are inconsistent with IADB's commitments to address the challenges of climate change and promote environmental and social sustainability, such as • Thermal coal mining or coal-fired power generation and associated facilities. • Upstream oil exploration and development projects. • Upstream gas exploration and development projects.
World Bank Group Energy Directions 2013	Strategy	2013	Five directions: • Focus on the Poor – Universal Access • Accelerate Efficiency Gains • Expand Renewable Energy • Create an Enabling Environment • Intensify Global Advocacy 　° Greenfield coal-fired power in exceptional cases only

Source: Asian Development Bank (formerly Sustainable Development and Climate Change Department).

APPENDIX 5
Results Framework and Theory of Change

Impact:

An inclusive, just, and affordable, low-carbon transition in Asia and the Pacific achieved.

Table A5.1: Results Framework and Theory of Change

Outcome	Outcome Indicators	Output	Output Indicators
Universal energy access including clean cooking and heating provided	• New households connected to electricity (number) • New electricity generation capacity installed (megawatts [MW]) • Transmission lines installed and/or upgraded (km) • Distribution lines installed and/or upgraded	Investments in energy access increased	Increasing share of committed energy access investments to total committed energy sector investments (baseline: 2020 figures)
Climate and disaster resilience in communities improved	• Greenhouse gas emission reduction (tons of carbon dioxide equivalent/year) • Additional installed renewable energy capacity (MW)	Climate finance in energy expanded	Increasing share of committed climate finance to total committed energy sector investments (baseline: 2020 figures)
Financially sustainable and affordable energy services achieved	• Entities with improved planning and management functions and financial sustainability (number) • Entities with improved service delivery (number)	Support for energy sector reforms and institutional development enhanced	Increasing share of committed financing for energy sector reforms and governance to total committed energy sector investments (baseline: 2020 figures)
Energy security and cross-border access to cleaner energy sources increased	• Clean energy capacity for cross-border power trade installed and/or improved (MW) • Regional or subregional mechanisms created or operationalized to enhance coordination and cooperation among DMCs in energy (number)	Investments in cross-border power trade and regional cooperation in energy increased	Increasing share of committed energy trade investments to total committed energy sector investments (baseline: 2020 figures)
Solution with magnified development impacts integrated	• People with strengthened climate and disaster resilience (number) • People benefiting from strengthened environmental sustainability (number)	Adaptation finance in energy increased	Increasing share of committed adaptation finance to total committed energy sector investments (baseline: 2020 figures)

Source: Asian Development Bank (formerly Sustainable Development and Climate Change Department).

www.ingramcontent.com/pod-product-compliance
Lightning Source LLC
Chambersburg PA
CBHW042035220326
41599CB00045BA/7404